AN EXPANDING SOCIETY

ERRATA

p. 28, lines 1 and 2

'the legitimate...secured', remove inverted commas.

lines 4 and 5

'I should deplore the day when the land lost its legitimate influence. But that day will never come, the land always must, and will, retain its legitimate influence.' (Peel, Hope, Feb. 21, 1850. *Hansard*, 3rd ser: Vol. 108, 1250.)

p. 44, line 5

Gladstone's wife was Catherine, daughter of Sir Stephen Glynne; her sister married George William, Lord Lyttelton.

p. 50, line 11

The words should rather be 'suggested and not requested'. My account of the incident is oversimplified, but its general significance is as stated. See A. W. Kinglake, *The Invasion of the Crimea* (6th Edition, 1883), Vol. II, p. 110.

p. 87, line 25

'Koenig'.

p. 181, line 29

'attach to the doctrine'.

G.K.C.

AN EXPANDING SOCIETY

Britain 1830-1900

G. S. R. KITSON CLARK

Reader in Constitutional History
University of Cambridge

CAMBRIDGE

AT THE UNIVERSITY PRESS

MELBOURNE UNIVERSITY PRESS

1967

PUBLISHED BY

THE SYNDICS OF THE CAMBRIDGE UNIVERSITY PRESS

Bentley House, 200 Euston Road, London, N.W.1
American Branch: 32 East 57th Street, New York, N.Y. 10022
published in Australia and New Zealand by

MELBOURNE UNIVERSITY PRESS

942.081
K62e

Dewey Decimal Classification Number 942.081
Library of Congress Catalogue Card Number 67-13257

Printed in Australia by Melbourne University Press

FOREWORD

GEORGE ERNEST MUELLER SCOTT, who from 1918 to 1924 was a member of Ormond College in the University of Melbourne, never lost interest in its well-being. He was a graduate of this University in medicine, and on his death left half the residue of his estate to the University of Melbourne, and half to this College. In his lifetime he had already made regular and substantial contributions to the College's Endowment Fund. Dr Scott's will leaves the Council a wide power of discretion, but at the same time indicates ways in which he hoped that the money might be used. Foremost among the objects listed was the establishment of a Fellowship or Fellowships at this College. In a codicil to his will Dr Scott declares 'By Fellowship herein I am intended to mean a lecturer of eminence in his subject of scholarship'.

It was with great satisfaction that this College learnt that the first holder of the George Scott Visiting Fellowship would be Dr George Kitson Clark, whose visit to Melbourne was also assisted by a grant from the Margaret Kiddle Fund, in the gift of the Professors of History in the University. During his time in Melbourne Dr Kitson Clark delivered lectures which form the basis of this book. Those who read it will now have the opportunity of gaining a fresh view of the position reached in historical study of nineteenth-century England, a period which deeply influenced the life and development of the State of Victoria and the shape and tenor of our community life.

This College is, and will remain, grateful to Dr Kitson Clark for giving us the distinction of his presence and mind, so that we were able worthily to inaugurate this Fellowship, and fulfil so adequately the intentions of our benefactor.

J. DAVIS McCAUGHEY
Master of Ormond College
9 May 1966

v

145 43

CONTENTS

INTRODUCTION

THIS BOOK is founded on the lectures which as George Scott Visiting Fellow I delivered at Ormond College in June and July 1964, and my first task is to thank as warmly as I can the Master and other members of the College for giving me this opportunity, and also for their unremitting kindness and friendliness to me throughout my visit. To this I would wish to add my thanks to my colleagues, if I may still presume to call them so, in the Department of History in the University of Melbourne. I would like to thank them for their cheerful companionship, and for all that they were prepared to do for me, and not least for the help they have given in getting this book published. I would like to feel that I still remained in some small way a member both of Ormond College and of the University of Melbourne.

Before I left for Australia I did not feel that it would be desirable to prepare lectures for an audience of whose nature and needs I was ignorant. I still think this was right, but it meant that I had to prepare what I had to say, when I reached Melbourne, without the help of my own library or the libraries of Trinity College and Cambridge University on all of which I am used to depend, while a rather full programme of visits and lectures left me less time than I would have desired to use the library facilities which were generously put at my disposal at Melbourne. The lectures had in fact to be composed to some extent under pressure and I had little time to do more than check facts and verify references. There may have been advantage in this. A sense of urgency is an effective tamer of inhibitions, and there may be considerable advantage in a man being forced to produce opinions upon which he might be tempted to hedge, or which he might keep to himself if he had been given time to develop doubts. But it is desirable that this work should be recognized for what it is, work produced to some extent in an extemporary fashion without much opportunity to revise or confirm it before delivery. Not, except in two cases, have I re-

vised them much for publication since I delivered them. The
lectures were given from notes and subsequently transcribed
from a tape recording. They needed therefore a certain amount
of editing and reshaping. But, except in two cases, they have
not I believe been fundamentally altered in the process, for I
thought that it was best to put them forward as they were given,
as far as that was possible.

The two exceptions are lectures 5 and 8 which have now
become the chapter on 'imperialism' and the chapter on 'the
modern state'. To the chapter on imperialism, on the advice of
scholars who read it in draft, I added passages to cover two points
which they thought it important to make. I did not revise it as
radically as I might have been tempted to do by the results of a
coincidence. After I had left England in 1964 the Cambridge
University Press published *Imperialism: The Story and Significance of a Political Word, 1840-1960* by R. Koebner and H. D.
Schmidt. This treats much the same problem that I have tried to
treat in my lecture, only with much more learning and after more
prolonged research than I have been able to apply to it. When I
conceived this lecture I was unaware of the existence of this
book. I have been long convinced of the importance of this
approach to this subject, indeed an address by me on this subject
had been printed in a journal as long ago as 1952. When I
actually composed this lecture, just before its delivery, I knew
of the book's existence and, in general terms of its argument, for
I had seen a review, but I had had no opportunity to read it.
Indeed I believe that no copies had as yet reached Australia. If
I had read it at that time no doubt what I produced would have
been different, though I am pleased to say that what I said seems
in many points to be confirmed by what the book establishes.
But it seems to me to be undesirable to rewrite what I had produced quite independently. I have therefore as far as what is
covered by this important work is concerned, left things exactly
as they were.

With regard to the last chapter the case is different. When I
returned to Cambridge I found that much work was going forward on this subject. Research students were working upon it,
and there was sufficient undergraduate interest in it to make it
desirable for me to take two series of classes on it in two succes-

sive terms. All this was a stimulus to thought and when in my editing of the transcribed tape recording I came to this lecture I found I could not bring myself to publish exactly what I had said the year before. I, therefore, completely rewrote it making, I am afraid, the chapter considerably longer than the lecture ever had been, though the lecture had been the longest of the series.

In doing this reconstruction one particular object seemed to be almost more important than anything else. When discussing this subject both with undergraduates, and with groups of people from outside Cambridge, I came to the conclusion that a clear minded approach to this subject was often impeded by the use of abstract phrases and general assumptions which, at least in the form in which they were normally understood, had no satisfactory relationship with reality. The best corrective to this tendency seemed to me to insert into any account of it as many concrete examples of what was being discussed as possible. I could not have done this when composing a lecture largely from memory at Melbourne, but I have tried to do it, perhaps to the point of tediousness, when re-writing it at Cambridge.

The rewriting of this lecture has put me under certain obligations. Any one who has any knowledge of the subject will realize how much I owe to those who have previously written about it, and in particular to Dr Oliver MacDonagh, to whom during his years in Cambridge I owed very much. I would also like to confess my debt to Dr Greenaway of the Science Museum from whom I first learnt of the importance of the Alkali Acts. But I would most particularly like to put on record how much I have learnt from three research students now working with me, from Roy Macleod, now working on a critical period in the development of public health in the twentieth century, but also, as a necessary preliminary, conducting a variety of enquiries into the relationship between the development of public administration and the development of the natural sciences in the nineteenth century; and also from Richard Johnson and Henry Roper, who are dealing with the problems of the Education Department. I feel confident that in the not very distant future they will publish work which will both shew how great is my obligation to them, and also carry the whole subject far beyond my competence.

It is invidious to single out any particular individuals from my colleagues in Melbourne, but two of them unavoidably stand out for special mention. Miss G. H. Williams organized the typing of the lectures, and did the most difficult parts herself. It was often, I am afraid, a most distasteful task. For much of the work all she had to go upon was the transcript of a tape recording most obscurely corrected by myself. Upon Dr F. B. Smith fell a large part of the labour which was the unavoidable result of the need to convert the lectures into a state suitable for printing after I had returned to England. He also helped to supply the lists of books and articles, which I hope will be of assistance to those who may use this book. My debt to him is very great indeed. Indeed I do not see how without the devoted help of Miss Williams and Dr Smith this book could ever have come out. I owe them both my warmest thanks. I must add that for any mistakes in the book I alone am wholly responsible.

G. KITSON CLARK

Trinity College, Cambridge
November 1965

NOTE ON AUTHORITIES AND
FURTHER READING

IT DOES NOT SEEM to be desirable to burden a book of this kind
with an array of footnotes, which indeed in the circumstances
in which much of it was composed it would have been very
difficult to supply. Nor would it be easy to equip so general a
book with an adequate bibliography which was not impossibly
long. However, there may be an advantage in adding a postscript
which would serve the double purpose of making suggestions for
further reading for those wishing to study the subject and of
giving some idea of the authorities upon which the work is
founded.

It will probably be best to divide this postscript into two sections, first a section discussing very shortly general background
reading, and then a section dealing with each chapter in turn.

This work is not intended to be a comprehensive account of
British history between 1830 and 1900, it does not even intend
to deal with all the matters which are immediately relevant to
the process of expansion. There is nothing in it for instance
about the problems of the accumulation of capital or about industrial growth. All that it intends to do is to suggest some lines
of thought upon particular aspects of this period. For this reason
this book is no substitute for a study of general works on the
nineteenth century, indeed, like other books of its sort it cannot
be properly understood without some knowledge of the general
background.

The trouble about all general books is that with the development of historical research and the realization of new insights
into historical processes they tend nowadays to get out of date
rather quickly. This tendency has, however, this result. If the
most modern books soon need supplement or correction, it is
equally convenient to use older books of merit if one remains
always prepared to reconsider their conclusions in the light of
more recent thought. In my view the most valuable book on

those parts of British nineteenth century history which it touches is still Élie Halévy, *Histoire du Peuple Anglais au XIX° Siècle* (in either French or English). The standard books which many people use are the relevant volumes of the *Oxford History of England,* both are good, particularly that by Ensor, but both are out of date and there is a great deal to be gained even now from older books of the full old-fashioned leisurely sort such as Spencer Walpole's *History of England.*

Possibly the most remarkable general book on British nineteenth century is G. M. Young's *Victorian England: Portrait of an Age,* a book of great charm and great penetration. In any study of nineteenth-century problems I would say it would be necessary to read G. M. Young at some point. With this advice it is necessary to give two warnings. Because of its fondness for obscure allusions and its lack of notes and references it is in some ways a tiresome book, and fairly often I have found that students to whom I have commended it have been made, for reasons I do not fully understand, extremely angry by it. Other teachers in other universities have had the same experience. The second warning is this. Young apparently habitually quoted from memory without, it would seem, often verifying his quotations. As a result he often misquotes, even from his favourite Tennyson. Sometimes, in my view, he also misremembers the significance of a passage he uses, and once at least he misnames the leading person in a story. None of this in my view really detracts from the value and charm of his work, supported as it was by an acute intelligence, a remarkable memory and reading so wide that I have never yet met a scholar who recognized all, or even most of, his allusions. But it means that his readers must be circumspect.

There are more modern general books which I would commend as being peculiarly relevant to the subjects with which this book tries to deal: Professor Asa Briggs, *The Age of Improvement,* Professor W. L. Burn, *The Age of Equipoise* and my own *Making of Victorian England* of which this book is in a way an extension.

There are of course many other books on particular subjects on Economic History, on Literary and Political History and a growing number of important biographies, all of which would help the understanding of the general history of this period. But it would go beyond the purposes of this postscript to name them except in so far as they relate to particular chapters.

The lists of books appended to each chapter are not intended as bibliographies of the material included in the chapter, but rather as guides to help the reader to follow up some of the points that are raised.

1

THE GENERAL APPROACH
SOCIAL, INTELLECTUAL, POLITICAL

MY FIRST TASK is to offer my profound thanks to the authorities
at Ormond College for my election to the Scott Fellowship, an
honour that I esteem the more since I am to be the first Scott
Fellow. Without doubt more eminent men will follow when I
have left, but no one will, ever be able to dispute with me the
honour of instituting the first fellowship, and I appreciate it very
much.

It is that fellowship which has enabled me to give this course;
and I wish, as the circumstances seem suitable, to start in Australia and work from there to Britain. It is suitable, but it is
dangerous since it entails my talking about something of which
my knowledge is limited, before an audience many of whom
will know a great deal about it, while all I have to offer as a
reason for this choice is that most shadowy and deceptive of
phantoms, an hypothesis based on an impression. It is, however,
a very strong impression. I realize now that it has been building
up in my mind for years, though it only became clear to me
when I arrived in Melbourne and saw your nineteenth-century
architecture, particularly the architecture of your churches and
chapels. I then recognized a feeling which came upon me two
years ago on my first trip to Pakistan and India. On the first
morning of my arrival I went for a walk and there, peeping at
me from behind the trees, was a building of unmistakable English Gothic architecture, utterly unsuited to that climate, utterly
unsuited to the surrounding architecture. And that recollection
carries me back to my first visits to Boston and Philadelphia,
when I taught for two terms in the University of Pennsylvania.
Again, when I went for my first walk I saw the same architecture, architecture of which the style and inspiration was unmis-
takably British, though mixed in those cities with more that was
of German or Italian origin.

I have gained from these memories the impression of a com-

1

mon civilization. It is an English-speaking culture, I may not call it British, since it must include the Irish; a culture with the same modes of thought, the same often, alas, rather deficient aesthetic standards; a culture which had been extended all over the world in the early and middle nineteenth century.

I need not say that this impression is not based only upon fancied resemblances in buildings. It is reinforced by other things, it is reinforced by the fact that many of the denominations which used the churches whose architecture impressed me were the same denominations as I could have found in Britain. Some of them were denominations which in the form they had assumed, were, I believe, peculiar to English-speaking countries, such as the Methodists, the Church of England, the Unitarians and the Baptists. Others were denominations whose origins lay more completely outside British history, such as the Presbyterians or the Roman Catholics, but even so this Presbyterianism had been strongly moulded by Scottish or Welsh influences; and the Catholicism I saw was often Irish Catholicism which is, I venture to say it with the deepest respect, not quite the same as that of the Catholicism of any other nation. All these people derived from the British Isles, many of them had kept up their connections with the British Isles, and they seem to have exported thence their prejudices and their principles. For instance quite recently I had the honour to take part in a large conference of Presbyterian ministers, and I was surprised to find that the Great Disruption, which I should have thought was a movement which arose from conditions peculiar to Scotland and the position of the landowners in Scotland, had been exported to these shores, and had had profound effects here, while the controversies in your history about state aid to Churches seem to have been exported, lock, stock and barrel, from the controversies of the England of the same period.

The same close connection appears in quite different things. While I was working in Philadelphia, I wrote an essay on popular romanticism, which subsequently appeared among the essays called *Studies in Social History* which we presented to George Trevelyan on his eightieth birthday. For this work I required access to a good many books in which people had been much interested in the 1830s and 1840s, and in which for good reason not many people have been interested since. They had all been published in Britain, and referred to British conditions, but it was possible for me to do the entire essay from books which I read in the University Library at Pennsylvania. They had been in Philadelphia in one library or another ever since their publication. I have no doubt the same books would be found in the public libraries in Melbourne. When I visited Chicago I met a member of the University of Chicago who was interested in the early theatre of Chicago and he told me that plays which I had been considering, which had been successes in Drury Lane, had appealed also to the same kind of audience in Chicago; I would like to make a similar comparison with the Melbourne theatre. I could go on indefinitely, I could go to the legacy of the common law, not only in positive law, but to ways of thought and terms of political language which you will find in every political controversy. I could go to the complexities of economic relationships and the resemblances in the patterns of commercial practice. But perhaps I have said enough to suggest that historical conception which some historian, younger and better skilled than myself, will, I hope, some day work out.

It is the conception of a great diaspora of the English-speaking people. They leave a common cradle. They go in widely different directions—to Australia, to New Zealand, in certain capacities to India, to South Africa, to Canada, to the United States, to the Argentine and even to Patagonia, where there is a colony of Welsh farmers. They are confronted by different conditions, they experience widely different fates, but they have so much in common, brought with them from their common origin, that you cannot understand any section of them completely unless you take account of the whole. It was a great movement of men and women comparable to the folk-wandering of the Germans who broke into the Roman Empire in the fifth century; it is also possibly comparable to the great folk-movement of the Arabs which bore the tide of Mohammedan conquest right across the world in the early Middle Ages. As in all cases of the folk-wandering, the forces behind it were various. There was, just as in the case of the Mohammedan conquest, a missionary instinct, in this case the missionary instinct either of Christians as Christians, or the missionary instinct of the people who felt that they had a civilization which was better than all the other civilizations of the world. There were also the temptations of power, in this case the possibilities offered by sea power, which made conquest and colonization relatively easy. But there was one force behind this movement which I should guess lay behind many of the great movements of people: the drive of hunger. In most cases something had caused a population somewhere to increase so fast that it could no longer be easily supported in its home grounds. Thus to the temptations to wander might be added the compulsion of necessity. A situation might develop in which men had to leave their homes or die, or be content to live a life not much different from death.

Some such compulsion was behind this wandering. From some point in the eighteenth century, the population of Britain had been increasing. In 1801 the population of England and Wales had probably reached nine million persons. The process went on. In 1851 the population of England and Wales was nearly eighteen million,—it had doubled or nearly doubled. In 1901 the population of England and Wales had gone up to about thirty-six million, it had nearly doubled again. There is a comparable increase in Scotland and in Ireland. It is calculated that in 1845 the population of Ireland numbered no less than 8,250,000 persons and that in 1851 if there had been no potato famine it would have been nine million persons. That is more than the whole population of Australia a hundred years later. These figures for England and Wales, Scotland, and Ireland probably meant that there were more people in the countries than they could reasonably support, for in 1801 even in England most of the people lived in the country. This meant that conditions in the country districts were bad and were deteriorating. They were very bad in parts of England at the beginning of the century where to the results of over-population were added the effects of enclosures and bad harvests. But they were much worse in Ireland. Ireland is naturally a poor country. It has little or no natural mineral wealth, much of the land is bog and so covered with peat that it is very difficult to use, and much is barren rock. Of course it had been misgoverned, and there is, no doubt, much to be said against Irish landlords, though much that has been said has been said in ignorance. But whatever landlords there had been, whatever the government might have done, nothing could have enabled Ireland to support between eight and nine million people in anything but the direst, most hopeless and most dangerous poverty. The only thing which kept them alive at all was the potato, and in the late summer of 1845, and in the winter of 1846 and in 1847 the potatoes were dug from the pits, stricken with disease, black, rotten and useless. Therefore many of the Irish were faced with the dilemma—go or die. It is calculated that above a million went and nearly a million died.

This is the pressure of population at its starkest. In more moderate form that pressure was being exerted all through the British Isles. It was not always the threat of actual starvation. It was more often felt by people who saw no hope of improvement in their condition. There was a whisper in the ear of people in all ranks of society, since the increase of population had affected all ranks of society, 'unless you wish never to improve your lot, unless you are content going to sink into a lower level, you must go, you must go, you must go'. Many listened to it, the intelligent labourer, the younger sons of small farmers, the graduates of Glasgow, Edinburgh and Trinity College, Dublin, who saw little chance of fruitfully employing their talents as medical men, lawyers or divines in the crowded land of their birth.

They had a good chance of improving their condition abroad largely because behind this movement there was another force equal in power to the population explosion. It is what is called the Industrial Revolution, that is, the application of mechanical invention and the methods of mass production to British industry. The revolution was going forward with increasing speed in Great Britain, from about 1780 on into the nineteenth century. This, in due course, supplied the transport which made emigration possible. It also kept the trade routes in action along which the emigrant ships might travel, but what was much more important than either of those things, it was this revolution which supplied the chances of employment in the countries of reception. It provided capital for their development, it provided a hungry demand for raw materials, for cotton from the southern States of the United States, for wool from Australia, for timber from Canada, and for gold from wherever it could be found, and in due course, for food wherever it could be produced most cheaply, all of which had to be paid for by the goods which the new machines were creating in increasing abundance. It was this that enabled the countries of reception to pass rapidly from the state of subsistence economy to more elaborate communities with a much richer mode of life, and it secured that this new world which was coming into existence was largely a world of cities, and not only a world of frontiersmen.

I have called what resulted from this movement a 'culture', that is a situation which develops when a number of peoples and nations exist at the same time maintaining the same spiritual and intellectual backgrounds, using the same forms of thought and, in this case, speaking the same language. It was by no means a political unity. I suppose that as many people settled outside the British Empire, as within it, nor was it by any means a union of hearts. Referring to Australia, Sir Keith Hancock writes, 'Men do not emigrate in despair, but in hope'. That may be so, but at the moment of their departure from their mother country they do not always go in peace. When a man leaves his native haunts he may have been inspired by hope, but he may also have been impelled to go by hunger, or distress, or frustration or injustice, and these experiences may make him not look back on those who controlled his own home with the warmest consideration and regard. There was indeed a great variety of attitudes. In the famous pre-Raphaelite picture, 'The Last of England', there is a young couple sitting together on the deck of an emigrant ship and looking backward with what seems to be puzzled misery at the gradual disappearance of that land which they had called home, but which had no place for them. Standing behind them there is a figure that I take to be an Irishman, who laughs at the disappearing country and shakes his fist. Where the English went the Irish went with them, and with both races went the bitter feud between the Irish on the one hand and the English and the Scots on the other.

This did not really mean the break-up of the culture by the intrusion of an alien element. Hate may divide it, but it does not separate. The Irish owe much more to their English-speaking environment than they would care to accept. It was a friend from the National University of Ireland who first taught me how many of the ideas of Irish nationalism derived from the English common law. But the presence of the Irish encouraged a tendency in the new societies which was to be important: a tendency towards, if not hostility to the old society, at least hostility to those who traditionally governed it. Of course it was not true of all the people in the new societies in the new reception areas: there were many who came to the new societies who had enjoyed satisfactory positions in the old order: there were more who valued the old order of things when they could attain a reasonable place in the society which embodied it. There were officials, there were clergy of the Church of England, there were half pay officers who settled abroad and with these there were many who might be called the gentry of aspiration, men and women who had not started as gentlefolk, but who very much wished to assume the role. For neither the English nor the Scots lost all their social foibles when crossing salt water, and where they went snobbery went also. Nevertheless, the way in which the society in the new reception areas was recruited, and the way it made its money, made it likely that many of those who formed it should view the governing classes of the old country, their habits, their values, their pretensions, with hostility and some contempt.

And this brings me to a point which may have been troubling some of my audience. They may have been troubled by the question, why in a course of lectures ostensibly on British history, have I indulged myself in so long a preface which might seem mainly to be about communities outside Britain. Of course I might have done this because I wanted to make the point that to understand the history of Australia you must also understand something of the history of Britain, as also of the history of Canada and the United States, and in matters of government, India and Ireland; for that I believe to be a true point. But I have had a simpler reason for what I have done. Great Britain, or parts of it, was also a reception area in the folk-wanderings I have described, and the communities which developed in Great Britain assumed all the characteristics of new communities.

To make this point clear, it is only necessary to consider the movements of the Irish. It is often assumed that under the impact of the potato famine, most of the emigrating Irish went to the United States of America. I do not believe this to be true. After all, it was much easier and cheaper for very poor people in very desperate circumstances to go to Liverpool or Glasgow or Cardiff, rather than to go to New York or Boston. It is said that in the famine years of 1845-7, no less than 400,000 Irishmen came to Britain, but that figure is doubtful. What is more certain is that in the census of 1851 there were living in Britain 733,866 persons who had been born in Ireland, 519,959 of whom lived in England, and that neglects the numbers who escaped being counted, which, the Irish being what they are, were I think fairly considerable. Of course, some of those may have been making England a mere port of call until they could scrape enough money together to go overseas. But it is worth considering that 1851, the census year, is three to four years after the famine, and that not a few who had come to England during the famine would have died, or gone overseas already. More significant is the fact that by 1861 the number of those in England who had been born in Ireland had increased to 601,634, and to that number must by now be added a very considerable number of Irish children born after arrival. So it seems clear that a very large number of the Irish had come to make their homes in England and Scotland, a conclusion which some knowledge of the modern social structure of many British cities would suggest.

But the Irish were not the only men and women to come to British cities in these years. In the first half of the nineteenth century British cities were growing rapidly. Indeed, considering the nature of their growth and the nature of what was produced, they were growing horribly. Between 1821 and 1831 the addition to the numbers of people in Great Britain living in towns of over 20,000 inhabitants was no less than 1,100,000 persons. Between 1831 and 1841 it was 1,270,000 persons. Between 1841 and 1851 the addition was 1,800,000 persons. These people did not all come from Ireland. They came from the highlands of Scotland, they came from the valleys and mountains of Wales, they came from the English and the Scottish countryside. It was often a countryside quite near the city, but in these matters distance may not matter. If a man or woman has to leave the sanctions of home—if such sanctions have existed—and the customary life that he and his ancestors have lived; if he has to leave these for a new life, new companions and a new way of making his living, then even if the new life is being lived in a town only thirty miles off, even if it is being lived near a mine in the next valley, he would be likely to be as much uprooted as if he had crossed the seas; and for illiterate or partially illiterate people, in periods when communication was still relatively difficult, the possibility of coming back or communicating backwards might not be very great.

There was therefore a new, uprooted population in the great cities of England and Scotland, as there was a new uprooted population in the great cities of America and in the great cities of Australia. In Britain also there was the development of new forms of wealth, outside the time-hallowed system of agricultural wealth. Of course, Britain had never been entirely agricultural. There had always been places like London and Bristol in which men with non-agricultural wealth had been powerful. But such places had been few, and such men were a relatively small portion of the community. Nor were they ever the people who really controlled its government. Moreover, new fortunes had not remained outside the old system for very long. During the course of English history it has always proved to be possible, more possible than in other countries, to absorb any great fortune into the establishment. Even in sixteenth-century England it was said to be easy to make gentlemen. In the early nineteenth century it was very easy for a rich man to make himself a gentleman. All you had to do was to buy an estate, send your son to the right school and there you were, or there at any rate he was. In this way the Baring family, the Peel family, the Gladstone family, were all absorbed into the governing classes of the country. But what was happening in the second quarter of the nineteenth century was too massive to be absorbed in this way. Great or moderate wealth developed in the hands of people who could not be absorbed or did not want to be adsorbed; and cutting across that society there was a division that was becoming difficult even for a wealthy man to cross, the division between Church and Dissent. Therefore in that England a society developed which was divorced from the life which had gone on before. It developed in great cities. Sometimes these were to all intents and purposes new. Sometimes they formed round the nucleus of an old town, but even then what was in effect a new community came into existence. Very often the boundaries of the newly-populated area were different, and the social structure that developed was different from what had existed before. Very often also the government had been in the hands of a group which excluded the new men who were coming to be important. In many cases the new towns had forms of government which were utterly unsuited to the new communities which were growing up; for instance, until the 1830s, Manchester was governed by a manorial court. In some cases, the nucleus of these new towns had been so minute and so unimportant that what came into being was in effect a new community; sometimes, as in Middlesbrough, practically nothing had previously existed on their sites. They were in fact all new communities and their cities; their natural leaders were outside the old conception of an ordered society, presided over by the nobility and gentry. And so the idea which I want to put before you first of all, is that Birmingham, Manchester, Liverpool, Leeds, Glasgow and the rest were indeed the first and for long perhaps the most outstanding creations of this great folk-wandering, and they were in many ways as intellectually remote from the old as if they were in Australia or America.

But there was a serious difference between their situation and that of their contemporaries overseas. They were intellectually remote, they were removed in sympathy from the older world which existed in Britain, but they were not physically remote. The old world of the old Britain was all around them in massive force. Only a few miles out of a manufacturing town you might well come to the estate, or even the seat, of a great territorial magnate. Perhaps the town was partly built on ground owned by such a territorial magnate, as for instance the Earl of Derby who owned quite lot of ground of cities in Lancashire. The old aristocratic society still ruled the Britain in which these new great cities flourished. It could tax their wealth in order to maintain what must seem to them the absurdities of the court, the outrageous corruptions of Parliament and the idle lives of the well-connected. It could frustrate their commerce by imposing a protective system, which, in the view of the leaders of the new society, existed largely to maintain the rents of the aristocracy. It could flaunt its insolence in their faces, exact its privileges, use its influence to job itself into positions in the army. Therefore such hostility towards the old aristocracy as might exist in the new areas which were being created overseas, was likely to exist with a greater intensity at home.

There were, in fact, in Britain two nations struggling in the bosom of one land—an old nation based upon the old nobility, upon the squires and upon the Established Church, and a new nation based upon commerce and industry, and in religion largely Dissenting. Perhaps the new nation might be called liberal and the old nation Whig or Tory, it does not matter which. It is to the conflict between this new liberal Britain and the old Britain of the Whigs and the Tories that I will turn next time.

Briggs, Asa, *Victorian Cities*. London, 1963.

Carrington, C. E., *The British Overseas; Exploits of a Nation of Shopkeepers*. Cambridge, 1950.

Connell, K. H., *The Population of Ireland, 1750-1845*. Oxford, 1950.

Carrothers, W. A., *Emigration from the British Isles, with Special Reference to the Development of the Overseas Dominions*. London, 1929, 1965.

Cowan, Helen I., *British Emigration to British North America*. Toronto, 1961.

Hansen, M. L., *Atlantic Migration 1607-1860; History of the Continuing Settlement of the United States*. Cambridge, Mass., 1941.

Knowles, L. and C. M., *The Economic Development of the British Overseas Empire*. London, 1924, 1936.

2

PARTY POLITICS AND GOVERNMENT POLICY—I

I SAID IN MY LAST LECTURE that I would turn next to the conflict between the new Britain and the old, and to do this it seems
best to start by considering the word 'liberal'; for that word was
to summarize, and by so doing to form, the philosophy of what
was new. Elie Halévy, the greatest historian of the British
people in the nineteenth century, gave it as his view that 'liberal'
as a political nickname came from the troubles in Spain which
followed the restoration of the Bourbon monarchy. In Spain, he
says, there were two parties, Liberales and Serviles. The Liberales were those who opposed the brutality of the reactionary
monarchy, the restored inquisition and the Church. The Serviles
were those who supported them. He believes that the term was
exported from Spain to England, still retaining in its first usage
an 'e' after the second 'l'. I'm not too happy about this. The word
is in pretty general political usage early in the century. In 1820
a young Tory statesman, Robert Peel, who had just come back
from a tour of duty in Ireland wrote to his friend Croker to say,
as well he might, that the tone of England was more 'liberal',
'to use an odious but intelligible phrase', than the policy of the
government. Even if the word came as a political nickname from
Spain, as a word it had a long English tradition behind it going
back to a date well before the nineteenth century. It is used in
the Authorized Version, a fact fully exploited by Nonconformist
chapels in the middle of the nineteenth century at election time.
It is also used by Shakespeare of the coarse language of shep-
herds, which was not of such use to them. There had been from
the Middle Ages onwards 'liberal' arts and 'liberal' professions.
Men had received a 'liberal' education and 'liberality' was used
as a general synonym for generosity. Whatever its immediate
origins these various English usages must have coloured its
political meaning.

Towards the middle of the nineteenth century possibly the
association which most profoundly affected the word 'liberal'

12

was the idea of liberty; this was particularly so when free trade had come to play so large a part in liberal philosophy. Liberalism as the creed of liberty could be applied to a variety of subjects which had a peculiar interest for the kind of people who were liberals. There was freedom of opinion, which meant to them opinion free from the intolerable shackles and privileges of the established Church. There was freedom for exchange in land, which meant land free from the encumbering settlements and the whole legal framework which existed to maintain intact the estates of the aristocracy. There was freedom for self-made men from the offence of hereditary privilege, freedom from the the arbitrary actions of the executive, freedom from the weight of taxation, freedom for nations abroad struggling under the yoke of foreign monarchs and aristocracies, and perhaps freedom also from those meddling philanthropists and busybodies who wished to interfere with the working conditions in a man's factory. All this could be fused into a working philosophy, a philosophy of liberty.

It could never be a wholly adequate philosophy, because, if you have any social values, freedom is never a sufficient answer to all problems. Apart from the expanding needs of government in any form of society there would always be helpless people on the hands of the public—people like children or negroes or Irishmen or sailors, who could not be trusted to look after themselves, and for whom therefore not freedom but active protection and control was needed. As a result, it was quite impossible to have a completely *laissez faire* state. Recent history had emphasized this fact. There had been in the sixteenth and seventeenth centuries a heavily regulated state in England, with wages, the price of beer, of bread and terms of employment all carefully controlled. People had ceased to believe in the value of such controls and in the eighteenth and nineteenth centuries these things had either fallen quietly into desuetude or the legislation which enforced them had been repealed. But it proved to be impossible to maintain a vacuum in this matter. A state which does nothing for anybody and lets everyone go his own way is virtually impossible. Before the last of the old legislation had been repealed, the first of the factory laws to protect children had come into existence, while there was no real break, from the Middle Ages onwards right up to the great Charter of 1854 in the laws dealing with seamen. These things could, however, all be dismissed as exceptions to the prevailing philosophy, the more easily as in most cases people did not realize how many exceptions were being permitted, or what they were portending. It was only after 1870 that collectivism began obviously to close in on freedom and to such an extent that a new conception of liberalism became necessary, if liberalism it could still be called. Before 1870 freedom from the interference of the state, freedom for competition in economic and spiritual matters had seemed to be for many Britons a perfectly adequate philosophy on which to base their society.

However, a term which is being actively used in politics, cannot be defined only in the terms of a political philosophy. It must take part of its meaning at any time from the political situation of the moment, from the tasks which have to be done and also, always, from the enemies that have to be faced. As a matter of fact, when Peel used this 'odious but intelligible' term in 1820, I do not think he was thinking about freedom. I think, from something he said in another letter, that he meant a tendency to give too little importance to the virtues of prescription, to the inherited values of existing institutions. In 1820 there were good reasons for this tendency. The electoral system of Great Britain was absurd and indefensible. Several constituencies had disappeared, or ought to have disappeared, under the effacing hand of time. Old Sarum was simply empty fields, Dunwich had disappeared under the sea and all that remained was two houses and half a church; yet each of these constituencies returned two members to Parliament. Other electorates had been made to serve the political needs of a neighbouring magnate, and had lost any possible justification they might have had. The civil service was used to find jobs for greedy politicians or for the dependents and relatives of the nobility and gentry, indeed the obsolete offices of bygone systems of government stretching back into the Middle Ages remained in existence to provide incomes for people who were properly connected and wished to live without working. The criminal law of England was the most bloodthirsty in Europe. There were about two hundred actions, prescribed by it, to which the death penalty was attached. The civil law under which the country laboured was in some points the most artificial system that has ever encumbered a civilized State; and as for equity, it is I think important to remember that the picture in *Bleak House* of the case of *Jarndyce* v. *Jarndyce* is literally true. There are on record cases, which went on in Chancery for twenty years, until all the estate involved had been completely consumed by lawyers' fees. The organization and discipline of the Church of England were indefensible, pluralism was rife, absenteeism habitual. In 1827 of 10,500 clergy of the Church of England 4,500 were absent from one living or other that they held. The Universities of Oxford and Cambridge were full of abuses; there were professors who did not lecture, heads of houses who enjoyed in addition high ecclesiastical office, life fellows who did nothing at all. You could get a degree in Cambridge, without examination, if you were a nobleman, or if you were a member of King's College. There were comparable abuses at Oxford.

Small wonder there were people who paid insufficient attention to the virtues of prescription, when what survived from the past seemed often to be so bad. Indeed what survived from the past might inflict serious inconveniences on a man in his own private life. It was against the Established Church that an ordinary man was most likely to bark his shins, if he did not conform to it, as a large body in the nation refused to do. A man who was a Dissenter, and not a Quaker or a Jew, would, before 1836, still have to be married in church. This was an unexpected result of Hardwicke's Marriage Act, but it was very much resented. When he was dead he could not, if he was a Dissenter, be buried in the parish churchyard, except possibly with Anglican rites. If the churchwardens and the vestry thought fit, he might be subjected to a church-rate to support the fabric of his parish church and the requisites for its worship. He might have to pay tithe. Till 1854 a Dissenter could not matriculate at Oxford, not till 1856 could he take a degree at Cambridge. Until 1828 the Test and Corporation Acts made it difficult for a Dissenter to undertake a corporate office in his own town. If of course he was a Roman Catholic also, he was subject to added disabilities, which largely excluded him altogether from the political life of the country.

That was, however, not mainly an English question but an Irish question, and a very serious one. In England and Wales it was the disabilities of the Protestant Dissenters which were important because they served to inflame and to define the opposition of many of those who for any reason were not part of the government. In a corporate borough an important citizen who found himself outside the ring which governed the town, which was often centred on the parish church, would be likely to adhere to what had been a Presbyterian, but was now an Unitarian chapel. Or he might be one of the people called Quakers, a small but very influential denomination, or possibly if he were a little lower in the social scale he might be a Congregationalist or a Baptist. A man who lived in the country and stood out against the domination of parson and squire was likely to be one of the determined groups of freeholders associated with the seventeenth-century Independent chapels that survived in the country districts and small towns of England. In each case he would feel the weight of the hand of the Established Church all the time.

There was, it is true, one great body of Nonconformists who in their lead were officially Tory, the Methodists, under their 'Pope', Jabez Bunting, who announced that Methodism hated democracy as much as it hated sin. But that attitude was not congenial to all the rank and file of the Methodists, indeed, it caused continual trouble in the Methodist body; while the evangelical revival itself could be one of the greatest sources of power behind the attack on the old order of things. In very many cases the revival gave force and spiritual awareness to the men of the new society, and to the bodies which were its most characteristic expression. The Congregationalists and the Baptists both caught fire from it early in the nineteenth century and enormously increased their numbers. To the left of the Methodists there developed a number of splinter sects which drove deep into the body of the working classes. This movement affected, and was affected by, the changes in the social system and as the century went forward there was a large and increasing body of Dissenters who looked with anger at the Established Church and all its works. They began to be vocal in the 1830s. In 1834 Stephens, a rebel Wesleyan, said: 'Ere long, the very existence of the established church will be like a tale that is told and will be remembered only for the moral evils which it has brought upon the country.' In 1841 Edward Miall, the Congregationalist, described the Established Church with great bitterness: 'The whole thing' said he 'is a stupendous money scheme carried on under false pretences—a bundle of vested rights, stamped for greater security with the sacred name of Christianity.' Or, he says more picturesquely in another passage: 'Trace the history of this or any other state church and almost every footstep plashes in the blood of man.'

Behind the Church loomed what Cobden called the 'booby squires' with their sporting rights, their local tyrannies, their electoral influence. Behind the squires were the Lords, splendid and intolerable, monopolizing all government, turning everything to their corrupt advantages, living, it was hoped and believed, lives of insolent uselessness and often, so also it was hoped and believed, behaving in a way that was a disgrace to their species. I do not think it is often realized how widespread and bitter in the first half of the nineteenth century was the dislike in England of the English nobility. It appears in the early speeches of Bright, it appears in stronger form in the propaganda of the Anti-Corn Law League, and it can be found in contemporary literature, particularly popular literature. It appears in Dickens, first in a characteristically crude form in *Nicholas Nickleby* in the persons of Sir Mulberry Hawk and Lord Verisopht. Then more subtly and delicately in the character of Sir Leicester Dedlock in *Bleak House*. Or in *Little Dorrit,* particularly in the magnificent chapter on the The Barnacles and the Circumlocution Office, which I believe is one of the most effective satirical passages in our language. It is, however, in his cruder satire that Dickens is most significant, for that is the way in which men saw this issue in the first half of the century. Theirs was a crude, harsh view and it should be seen for what it was. Indeed it is necessary here, as it is so often, to look for the feelings of ordinary men and women in literature which it is now impossible to take seriously, such as the Victorian melodrama and the popular novel. The bold, bad baronet of the Victorian melodrama, who spends his life oppressing the villagers, guarding the guilty secret that he is not the legitimate, or eldest, son of his father and seducing or attempting to seduce the daughters of the poor, is not a figure any historian is likely to take as very good evidence for the kind of man likely to be found in any country-house. But it is important to remember that this kind of thing was what audiences at that time took seriously and relished, and if the events and people did not actually correspond to anything in their experience at least they accepted them as probable. The same thing is probably true of the novels of a man like Reynolds, author, publisher and newspaper proprietor. He made it his business in his novels to expose the evils of the licentious aristocracy. The books are, of course, ridiculous, but their great popularity is significant. It need hardly be said that in real life the nobility were not so outrageous, nor were they so picturesque. There were and there continued to be some very bad men among them like Lord Hertford, there were some very insolent men like Lord Cardigan and there were careless and trivial men who wasted their resources on foolish ambitions like the Duke of Buckingham. But it has to be admitted that there were many respectable peers and peeresses, particularly among those who were influenced by the evangelical revival. There were also among the nobility some very valuable public servants. But I do not think any of this matters. What matters is that this was what men felt about the peerage and it had enough truth behind it to give it force and effect.

Therefore, the Britain of the first quarter of the nineteenth century is a country of corrupt, unpopular institutions in which drastic changes could not be avoided. The people who continued to flourish, the things which happened every day in Britain were often condemned alike by the best modern thought of the time and the feelings, reasonable or ignorant, of a considerable part of the population. There was developing in the country a new society outside the social hierarchy and relatively unrepresented in the seat of government. To make matters more urgent, in the years 1815-20 there was widespread and bitterly resented distress, coming as the result of the aftermath of war and the hasty demobilization of the armed forces, and this was made worse by very high food prices. A drastic change was inevitable and, so it seemed, might come suddenly. The only problem was how it would come.

Upon that might depend the answer to the question, what kind of Britain would emerge from the change. However, in considering that issue it would be as well not to underestimate the strength of the fortress to be taken. The old institutions of the nation might be uncouth, but they were not feeble. The technique of managing the King's government in collaboration with Parliament had been worked out through the centuries. Certainly it needed both aristocratic influence and corruption to make it go. But it did go. It supplied the government with money. It had never reached the kind of futility and bankruptcy which characterized the French government before the Revolution; indeed it had proved itself to be strong enough to fight the Revolution, to defeat Napoleon and to come out at the other end of the war solvent. The electoral system, intolerable as it was, did support effective government. More than that, it carried the roots of the government out far into the country. To secure elections the votes of a good many people were required. Sometimes they were given as a matter of duty, as by a tenant to the nominee of a landlord or by a government employee to the government candidate. Sometimes they were given for a recompense. In the case of a small man, this might be simply a money bribe; in more cases it was a job. The desire for offices of profit under government and the belief that they could somehow be obtained by asking the right politician in the right way seems to have pervaded all classes. The enjoyment of patronage and hopes for patronage kept a fairly large number of people in the country ultimately in a common allegiance to the professional politicians who supported the King's government. This, however, was not the only support that the King's government needed. It needed also the support of the independent country gentlemen, who in normal times and when not particularly aggrieved, supported the King as a matter of duty, both in Parliament and in keeping order in their countries.

Government therefore had to have broad foundations in a society that was both virile and self-confident. What that society admired greatly was a quality it called 'bottom'. It was 'bottom' that made a man lead a hunting field over a five-bar gate. It was 'bottom' that made a man stand fire in a duel, and it was 'bottom' that made a man like George Bentinck control a racing mob with a light switch and a raucous voice. It was 'bottom' which enabled a man to stand up on the hustings and speak his mind while as a matter of routine the mob pelted him with any filth that lay at hand, and it was 'bottom' that would lead a man to read the Riot Act with the stones whistling round his beaver hat or defend his house against an intrusive mob.

Such a society was not likely to yield easily, and its bulwarks were not likely to be carried by force. Various historians have asked why in these difficult years there was no revolution in Britain. I believe myself that part of the answer is simple. More power would have had to be deployed to overthrow the government than any popular uprising would be likely to develop. A revolution is an appeal to force, and a disciplined force, even with the clumsy weapons of those days, if it is loyal and used with determination and skill is easily the match for an undisciplined mob however numerous and angry. In 1839 three thousand miners poured into Newport to rescue some Chartist prisoners. They were met by twenty-two soldiers firing volleys, and driven back in confusion.

Certainly there never seems to have been a moment when the government of Britain had not, using the army, the yeomanry and the magistrates, far more than enough force to contain anything which might come against it. And in the last resort, however unpopular it might be, the government had on it side most of the people that mattered. Revolutions cause damage and danger and, however bad the government may have seemed, most men who had anything to lose preferred order to the danger of what had happened in France. Consequently whenever the danger seemed real, responsible opinion, however discontented, however strongly it had been in opposition, rallied to the cause of order.

But this still leaves my original question unanswered. How was this ancient society to be changed, for changed it must be? As far as the first half of the century goes there seem to be two answers to that question. One begins to be effective in 1822 and remains important all through the century; the other affects the years of crisis 1827 to 1832.

The first is this. Even if this society were not to be forced it could be penetrated by ideas. With all its defects and in spite of a rather oppressive law of libel, British society was based on free discussion. There was on the whole, with certain exceptions, free discussion in the press. There was a fairly large body of controversial literature. There was free discussion in the learned journals of the day; and there was, continually, free discussion in both Houses of Parliament. In those Houses of Parliament any government, however broadly it might be based on corruption and influence, had to explain its actions and had to defend them. From very early in the century enlightened ideas were clearly gaining ground in the House of Commons. Members of the House began to listen to those who wanted to reform the criminal law; indeed that task would have been put in hand earlier in the century if it had not been for certain bloody-minded judges in the House of Lords. In 1807 they abolished the slave-trade. They moved towards the emancipation of the Roman Catholics from the disabilities under which they laboured, though old-fashioned religious people in the country thought that such an action would be peculiarly blasphemous and would put a period to Britain's greatness.

But at first the ministry seemed unable to follow suit. In the years that followed the war they were in great difficulties. They had no secure control of the House of Commons and they were not sure they could control the country. 1817 seemed to be a very dangerous year. In 1819 there was Peterloo and the fears that led to the Six Acts. In 1820 when George IV came to the throne he cast the ministry into the mire by making them initiate divorce proceedings against his wife. In 1822 the unhappy Castlereagh, worried out of his mind by blackmail, committed suicide. But after 1822 there was a change. It was not a change of government such as we would expect with one party taking the place of another party; indeed there was no party system then, as we understand the party system. All there was, was the organization of the King's government with, outside it or inside it, groups of politicians working together. The shadowy words, 'Whig' and 'Tory' can be used to describe some of these groups; they are words which sometimes to some people meant a good deal, and sometimes meant precious little. But they do not clearly divide politicians into two well defined bodies. The complexion of the government could alter through new groups and new individuals joining it, although there was no change in the party name people might give it, and the Prime Minister remained the same as before. That is what happened in 1822. The Prime Minister, Lord Liverpool, remained in his place, but the men he brought into the ministry liberalized its policy. Canning liberalized the foreign policy and Huskisson the fiscal policy of the country, substituting for the confusions of the past a rational policy of protection, while Robert Peel as Home Secretary undertook a very conservative reform of the criminal law.

This period of so-called Tory reform lasted until Lord Liverpool had a stroke in 1827, and a period of crisis began. It started by the ministry breaking up. Canning was chosen to succeed Liverpool, and Peel and the Duke of Wellington retired because the Duke would not serve under Canning, nor Peel under someone pledged to Catholic emancipation, to which he was steadfastly opposed. Then Canning died, and Goderich, the most feeble Prime Minister the country has ever had, was appointed in his place but did not even meet Parliament. The Duke had to come back as Prime Minister with Peel as his most important minister. It was not a position for which the Duke of Wellington, with all his virtues, was well fitted. Neither political penetration nor flexibility of mind had been granted to him and he was soon in trouble. He could not manage to keep Canning's followers in the ministry. In 1828 he was faced with a very ugly situation in Ireland. O'Connell, the great Irish Roman Catholic leader, developed so extensive an agitation that the government seemed to be faced with the alternatives of either granting Catholic emancipation or facing civil war, and on this occasion it seemed possible that the army might not be loyal, for a very large number of the rank and file were Irish Roman Catholics. The House of Commons had passed a resolution in favour of emancipation, and the Clare election had proved that the government could not risk a dissolution. In fact, emancipation was inevitable, and only Peel and the Duke could get it past the King and the House of Lords. They did their duty and put in through in 1829, although it was a measure which the Duke did not like and which Peel had always opposed. Many of their followers believed that to emancipate the Catholics was a vile betrayal of the principles of the constitution.

In this way there developed a situation which provided the second answer to the question how the change in the old constitution was to begin. In 1830 a number of the country gentlemen, upon whom the government counted, defected. They did this not only because they were angry at the concession of emancipation, but also because they believed that the government were indifferent to the condition of agriculture. Since 1813 prices had been falling. The government had, it is true, passed a Bill for the protection of corn in 1815; but that Act had not secured the price it had been intended to guarantee, and when the government had revised protection it had always been in a downward direction. More than this, the government had accepted from the economists the policy of return to a gold-based currency which had inflicted on agriculture the results of severe deflation, and they had refused to repeal the malt tax which was held, I think falsely, to press particularly hardly on agriculture. Therefore in 1829 and 1830, to the mystification of the Duke, the country gentlemen tended to turn against him. In 1830 there was a general election following the death of George IV. When Parliament reassembled in November of that year a complicated situation developed which it was beyond the Duke's political capacity to control. He had to face a demand for Parliamentary reform, and the continued hostility of the Protestants and the agriculturalists. He could have recruited additional liberal Tories for his ministry but failed to do so. When Parliament met he rejected Parliamentary reform with absurd and unnecessary emphasis. Consequently his government was defeated in the House of Commons and he resigned in a huff.

The Duke's defeat in 1830 is a landmark in British history. For one thing, this is the end of the old conception that ministers were primarily the servants of the King. The King's government had been defeated in the House of Commons on several earlier occasions and driven from office. George III had lost the ministers of his choice in 1782 and 1783. But in 1783 he was able to expel those who had been intruded on him and put in the younger Pitt. William IV was never able to do this. He would probably have liked to get rid of Earl Grey in 1831 or 1832, but he could not do so. In 1834 he tried to install Sir Robert Peel but could not keep him in office. Something which had been an inherent part of the constitution from time immemorial had disappeared. But the Duke's resignation had another result equally important. He was succeeded by Earl Grey, who was pledged to the reform of Parliament and who was able to pass the Reform Bill of 1832, the Bill which broke into the old Parliamentary system, got rid of the worst absurdities and enfranchised a number of manufacturing towns.

It is at this point that party politics start. Lord Grey's ministry was not at first a party ministry. It was a rag-bag of all men in opposition to the Duke, including some obvious Tories. However, because it proposed and passed into law the Reform Bill of 1832 it gained a popularity which made it so strong that the King could not get rid of it. It gained, further, the character of a Whig or Reforming ministry, so that it came to depend, as does a modern party ministry, on organized support in the House of Commons and the country and not on the King's favour. On the other side also there was a significant development. The Reform Bill crisis terrified the Tories, or as they now wished to call themselves, Conservatives. Croker, Peel's friend, told Peel after the Bill was passed that he saw the 'appalling vision of a bloody anarchy striding' towards him. The Duke of Wellington talked about revolution, and was afraid that the government would pass into the hands of the middle class, some of whom he believed were Socinians and others atheists. When Peel retired in 1835 after his abortive attempt at a ministry, old gentlemen begged him to hang on a little longer, saying that they were prepared to share his scaffold if things went wrong. Spurred on by these fears, therefore, the Conservatives built up a formidable party in opposition under his leadership. They recruited it from faithful Tories, frightened Whigs and repentant agriculturists, who soon found that they got as little relief from Whigs as they had done from the Tories. Since several of the men who retired with the Duke of Wellington had had the task of organizing the King's government, they were able to use the same techniques to organize the opposition. This indeed is probably the first opposition party to have a permanent organization which covered the whole country as does a modern party. At the centre they had an agent, Bonham, a party club, the Carlton, and a party fund; in the different constituencies they used local agents, normally solicitors, and local party associations to keep an eye on the register; and in 1841 they came into power as a modern party does, as a result of a long political campaign and, on this occasion, against the wishes of the Sovereign.

Here, then, there seems to be at last a breach in the fortifications. There has been a Reform Bill and party politics have begun. The new order of things has started, and with it, no doubt, the transference of power from one class to another. But in fact there has been very little transference of power. What has happened is a notable example of the technique that was to keep the middle classes out of power till three-quarters of the century were over. It was the technique of making obvious concessions, of granting liberal and humane reforms, while the old ruling classes kept the essentials of power under their hand. The Reform Bill was a necessary concession. It had enfranchised a number of towns which sooner or later had to be enfranchised. It gave votes to 'ten-pound' householders and thus enfranchised many members of the middle class who sooner or later would have had to be given votes. But it left in existence an overwhelming number of boroughs which were still under aristocratic control. It actually increased the votes for the counties and upheld the integrity of the counties by enfranchising manufacturing towns, the voters from which would otherwise have probably captured the county in which they lived. As a result, after 1832 politics in many places were controlled by the same people, or the same kind of people, who had controlled them before 1830, and the new party game which had started was not one in which the middle classes were called upon to play any great part.

These facts were realized and resented, and at the end of the thirties, there was launched a carefully organized attack on the aristocratic position through the agency of the Anti-Corn Law League. There were two reasons why the League arose when it did. Richard Cobden in 1837 and 1838 realized that earlier forms of radicalism had failed because they had been too diffuse in the number of objects they had pursued, and he felt that the proper thing to do was to concentrate on one object—the repeal of the laws which put a duty on corn and other provisions. However, it was also true that in the desperate depression which lasted from 1838 till 1843 it seemed to manufacturers and to others that the repeal of the Corn Laws was necessary to save British industry, and to save the British people from starvation. But whatever its origins, the campaign against the Corn Laws developed into a wild attack on the aristocracy, who were, in fact, not the major opponents of the repeal. In 1841 and 1842 the Anti-Corn Law League talked of revolution; it was not, it is true, revolution which they themselves were going to start, but it would be a revolution which they thought would be justified and which they would not oppose, a revolution upon which some of them changed their minds when rioting did start in the summer of 1842. They called Peel a murderer, and he thought they threatened to murder him. In fact they used all the gestures which it is proper to use when attacking pampered aristocrats battening on the hunger of the poor. But though the propaganda of the Anti-Corn Law League was violent, its organization was very remarkable and so was the talent, and the money, it had at its disposal. It had as its head Richard Cobden, perhaps the best political tactician of the century. It had the use of Bright, one of the greatest orators that have spoken the English language. It was able at the same time to make a fervent appeal to religious sanctions and to use its money and its organization to manipulate the parliamentary registers so that Protectionists lost their votes.

It appeared to succeed. In 1846 the Corn Laws were repealed. But that appearance was deceptive. It did, indeed, deceive many, including many who were prominent in the agitation of the League, who repeatedly tried the same tactics and never brought them off. The division lists at the time of the repeal disclose the fact that the number of votes which Cobden could control in the House of Commons could never have come near to repealing the Corn Laws. The Laws were repealed, partly because the Whig leader, Lord John Russell, was in favour of repeal, but mainly because the Conservative leader, Sir Robert Peel, had determined that they should go.

As far as Peel was concerned the repeal of the Corn Laws was in fact simply the continuation of the policy of the King's government before 1830. It is true that in 1841 Peel had come into office as Prime Minister as the result of the victory of a

party which contained a very large number of agricultural protectionists whose chief object was to retain the Corn Laws. But
he could not see himself as a minister appointed by a party. He
saw himself as a Minister of the Crown, as he had been before
1830, with a duty not to pay too much attention to what he
repeatedly called 'mere party considerations'. Before the Duke of
Wellington's government was defeated in the House of Commons, in 1830, they had been considering the imposition of an
income tax, which would have enabled them to cut indirect taxation and thus relieve the poor and encourage commerce. They
could not follow up this proposal because they were defeated
too soon and the Whigs were not good enough financiers to put
the scheme into effect. As soon as Peel got back into office in
1841 he took up that discussion almost as if he had never put
it down. It is perfectly true that the income tax was to be imposed in 1842 primarily to balance the budget, and to satisfy
an urgent financial necessity. But when Peel discussed the matter with Herries, who had been a minister in 1830, it seems clear
that both were thinking back to the earlier discussions, and when
Peel did impose his income tax it did enable him to make drastic
cuts in the duties on articles of consumption, and so to pursue
the policy which he believed was the proper way of relieving
distress, of making England a 'cheap country to live in'.

The policy seemed to be successful, and in 1845 he repeated
it again. It was a policy which would have led inevitably to his
repeal of the Corn Laws if there had been no prompting from
Cobden and no League to jog his elbow. It is true that in 1845
the decision to repeal was forced upon him by the Irish potato
famine. It is true that in doing what he did he had regard to the
agitation of the League: statesmen of the old school always had
to have regard to the feeling of the country. But it is also true
that he did not repeal the Corn Laws until he had assured himself, after very careful enquiries, that agriculture did not need
the protection of the Corn Laws, and would be better without it.
Indeed after he had been driven from office, within about a
month of his death, he told the country gentlemen in the House
of Commons with, I believe, absolute sincerity, that he had repealed the Corn Laws in order to remove from agriculture a
useless encumbrance, which was obviously felt as a bitter griev-

see
errata
page

ance by a large part of the country, in order that 'the legitimate influence of the country gentry should be secured'. This he felt he had done, and he said in a burst of confidence to the country gentry in the House of Commons: 'The land always will retain its legitimate influence.'

For twenty years it looked as if he had been right: for twenty years agriculture enjoyed a prosperity comparable to industry; for twenty years the country gentry legitimately influenced the elections in counties and small towns; for twenty years the nobility legitimately influenced the making of governments; for twenty years both gentry and nobility legitimately influenced the distribution of patronage in the civil service. All this, naturally, aroused great exasperation in John Bright, who had hoped for a real Reform Bill immediately after 1848: and so, I am sorry to say, in his haste he called the electoral system which was subject to all this legitimate influence 'a sham', which concealed the domination of the country by the titled and proprietary classes. But for twenty years he agitated fruitlessly against it, for the next Reform Bill was not till 1867. They were not, of course, even as regards reform, valueless years: very much that was important was done. But the moral of what had happened was this. The technique which had appeared in the passing of the first Reform Bill had been applied successfully to the dangerous problem of the Corn Laws. An apparent concession of great value had been made. By removing grievances, by passing reforms, by viewing carefully the opinion of the country, and yet by keeping in their hands the reality of power, the nobility and gentry contrived to govern England for three-quarters of the nineteenth century. In fact, till well after the first half of that century the situation of Britain still poses a question: When was there to be a change in the constitution which would also mean a transference of power? With that question I will deal next time.

Clark, G. S. R. Kitson, 'Hunger and Politics in 1842', *Journal of Modern History*, vol. xxv, no. 4, 1953.
——, 'The Electorate and the Repeal of the Corn Laws', *Transactions* of the Royal Historical Society, fifth series, vol. i, 1951.

Clark, G. S. R. Kitson, 'The Repeal of the Corn Laws and the Politics of the Forties', *Economic History Review*, second series, vol. ɪv, no. 1, 1951.

——, *Peel and the Conservative Party: A Study in Party Politics 1832-1841*. Second ed. London, 1964.

Gash, Norman, *Politics in the Age of Peel: A Study in the Technique of Parliamentary Representation 1830-1850*. London, 1953.

——, *Mr. Secretary Peel: The Life of Sir Robert Peel to 1830*. London, 1961.

——, 'Reaction and Reconstruction in English Politics, 1832-1852*. Oxford, 1965.

McCord, Norman, *The Anti-Corn Law League 1838-1846*. London, 1958.

Thompson, E. P., *The Making of the English Working Class*. London, 1963.

White, R. J., *Waterloo to Peterloo*. London, 1957.

Note: On the origins of the word 'Liberal' as a party label, see Élie Halévy, *History of the English People in the Nineteenth Century*, vol. 2, 'The Liberal Awakening, 1815-1830', pp. 81-2, n. 1, of the paperback edition, London, 1961. See also, Isaiah, xxxii. 5, 8 and *Hamlet*, iv, 7, 171.

3

PARTY POLITICS AND GOVERNMENT POLICY—II

I ENDED MY LAST LECTURE by saying that during the twenty years that followed the repeal of the Corn Laws what was old in England governed what was new. But I would not have you believe that all that time there was acute tension between them. It is quite true that during most of that period there was considerable tension between the Church of England and the Nonconformists. It is also true that Bright continued his attack on the titled and proprietary classes. Even here, the comradeship of the House of Commons and a broadened social experience seemed to have taken away some of the edge of his bitterness, and Bright in these years was rather a lonely, frustrated figure in the world of politics. Now that the Corn Laws were repealed, Cobden became less inclined to continue his attack on the aristocracy. The Anti-Corn Law League was dissolved as soon as the battle was over, only to come into existence briefly in 1847 when it looked as if there would be a revival of protection. The effective demand for extensive electoral reform died down. It was not that the electoral arrangements of the country were satisfactory—most intelligent men agreed that they were not, but the pressure behind the demand for reform died off, and successive ministers only fiddled with the subject. Reform Bills were introduced, they were debated endlessly and earnestly by members discussing what sections of the working class could be safely admitted into the electorate, and they were dropped without being passed into law.

One reason for this relaxation was the emollient effect of prosperity. Between 1847 and 1867 was the period of Britain's economic supremacy. The seeds of future difficulty were being sown in the development of the industrial revolution abroad, and in Britain's increasing neglect of the use of applied science, particularly of chemistry. But it was going to be some years before those seeds bore fruit, and during this whole period, there was, in general, increasing prosperity. Now and again, of course, there were difficulties, through over-eagerness and speculation. There was the collapse of the railway boom in 1847, something of a financial crisis in 1857, and the Overend Gurney crash in 1866. There were periods of great distress such as that caused by the cotton famine in Lancashire during the American Civil War. But in general the movement towards better conditions was continuous. It affected most classes of the country, except those at the bottom of the economic scale, and made men, at least for the moment, more satisfied with the positions they occupied in society.

It has indeed been noticed by historians that in working class movements in the twenty or thirty years that follow 1850, there is a change from the famished, desperate, half revolutionary movements of the 1830s and 1840s. Those earlier movements had been movements of men who could see no chance of betterment except through a drastic reconstruction of society. Now they might look forward to a change in society in the remote future, but they realized that before that day arrived there was much to be gained by the practical pursuit of limited objectives. This was implied in the change from Chartism to practical trade unionism and it made the working classes a much more important and effective section of the community. But one could follow this change of attitude all up the social scale; many people are pleased with what they have achieved in the past, and look forward with some confidence to improving their condition.

That does not mean that the contest between old and new had come to an end, but it does mean that there was some blurring of the edges. As people became more prosperous, they began to ape the upper class, they began to send their sons to public schools, which were being developed partly to meet that demand. They began to use Oxford and Cambridge, which after 1854 and 1856 gave degrees to Dissenters. This blurring was going to be important. It was going to lead to greater unity among the wealthier classes, and it was probably not going to lead to greater effectiveness among the leaders of industry, because the training at Oxford and Cambridge was largely traditional. At Cambridge it was mathematical and classical, the mathematics being very old-fashioned. At Oxford it was philosophical and classical, and in both, science was either relegated to a few specialists who were particularly interested, or else depressed to be the last resort of the desperate. 'I have been allowed the general and my reverend tutor thinks I shall have to take to science, which is commonly called stinks.'

The ordinary training at Oxford and Cambridge was, however, going to be important in another context. For this period saw the full development of what was in a way a new and important class of society, neither wholly committed to the old way of life, nor really a product of the new, the professional class. One of the important social tendencies of the eighteenth and nineteenth centuries was the establishment of the organized professions. The barristers had for long been organized in the Inns of Court, but now their training became better regulated, their position in society more definite, they probably increased in numbers, and new and very profitable lines of work developed in such things as the work of the Parliamentary Bar. It is, indeed, worth while to remember, that one of the reasons for the high capital cost of the British Railways was the immense legal expenses which they incurred in getting their Bills through Parliament. At the same time other professions emerged or were consolidated. There had in the past been no medical profession as such: there had been physicians, who were gentlemen, and apothecaries, who were not, and there were the surgeons who were often a pretty rough lot. In the nineteenth century all these were consolidated into one single, much respected profession, a process which was completed by the Medical Act of 1858. The same thing occurred with the solicitors, who were eventually organized as a profession under the Law Society with the sanction of a series of Solicitors' Acts. In roughly the same period first the civil and then the mechanical engineers organized themselves. The architects and the accountants were gradually to become a profession, and to these must be added the profession of the authors, many of whom were freed by the chance of making money by the mass production of their books from the miserable conditions that had prevailed in Grub Street or the degrading dependence on a patron.

The leading men of these professions and those who associated with them, were largely congregated in London, and there they created a society or class which was smaller than

either the old aristocratic society or the new society of the provinces, but which was much more important than its size would
warrant. It was important for a good many reasons. Much of the
intellectual life of the country passed through its hands. For
instance, this was the age of the great magazines, such as the
Edinburgh Review, or the *Quarterly Review*, or *Blackwood's
Edinburgh Magazine*, or *Fraser's Magazine*, or *The Economist*,
or that scourge of Nonconformists, the *Saturday Review*, and
there were others soon to appear. They carried articles of very
considerable literary and intellectual distinction, and gave space
to some of the important controversies of the day. It was largely
from this society, indeed in due course very largely from men
trained at Oxford, particularly Balliol, that for good and ill the
new all important advisory civil service was to be built up.

On the whole the members of this class, with the possible
exception of the mechanical engineers, were considered to be
gentlemen. It was largely fed from the Universities, probably
increasingly from Oxford and Cambridge when these were reformed and increased in size. For this reason probably most of
the professional men were inclined to be Church of England or
agnostic, but seldom Nonconformist unless they might be Unitarian. This fact was indeed one of things which cut them
off from the teeming life of the provinces, a life they were apt
to despise judging by the tone of the *Saturday Review* which
was probably their liveliest paper. In order, however, to understand them properly, it is best to look at the most formidable
monuments they have left behind them. One can say of a great
number of Englishmen—'by their Clubs ye shall know them'.
The development of the social club in London in the nineteenth
century is significant for a good many reasons, but it is particularly significant as evidence of the growth, prosperity and
nature of the body of people to whom I am referring. It is, indeed, remarkable that there grew up no less than three clubs to
cater for members of the old Universities, the Oxford and the
Cambridge Club, the United University and the New University. But there are other relevant clubs. There was for instance
the Garrick where Dickens and Thackeray started their feud,
and the Athenaeum where they were reconciled. The appointments of these clubs still seem to say much about the people

who frequented them. The comfortable chairs, the ample libraries, the not unreasonable cuisine and cellar, the general air of ease and unostentatious self-confidence—all seem to express forcibly the age and society that had developed.

But perhaps it is easier to see an age and a group mirrored not in an institution but in a man, and for me the image of that society always seems to be best epitomized in a relatively minor figure, Charles Stuart Calverley. His career is in many ways typical. He was a brilliant classical scholar, as scholarship went in that day, a fellow of Christ's College, Cambridge. This led, as it so often did, to a successful career at the Bar, cut short in this case by an early death. He was also the author of some of the best light verse in the language, and it is the absence of malice as also the absence of any serious satiric intention, even in the brilliant parody of Browning, which seems to express the ethos of the society that produced him. This seems to be confirmed by his picture, the ample beard, the leonine, rather tousled head of longish hair, the very comfortable easy clothes; these things seem to me to be true symbol of the easy, relaxed, self-confident culture that had come into existence in London in the 1850s and 1860s.

There are of course more significant and familiar figures in this epoch: the novelist Anthony Trollope, the effective and powerful barrister and essay writer, James Fitzjames Stephen and his brother Leslie, the fastidious Matthew Arnold, Clough the disappointed, or Tom Hughes the pugilistic Christian Socialist, and above all, the most influential member of this society and the most typical, Walter Bagehot. Indeed it is the contrast between the urbane and practical politics of Walter Bagehot and the typical creeds of the earlier nineteenth century which most deeply reflects the intellectual change that had taken place. The typical creeds of the early nineteenth century are Benthamism and Evangelical Christianity. Both are poles apart in their intellectual postulates, but in their methods of thought and in their practical results they are very much the same. In each case a hard dogmatic position is chosen and adhered to without the slightest concession to the fact that it is necessary sometimes to respect other people's opinions, and the implications of that postion are put into effect remorselessly and coldly. They were

fit creeds for a period of emotional tension and fanaticism. They
had been useful creeds. The nineteenth century started with the
attacks by the Evangelicals on slavery and the Benthamites on
the stupidity of the law. It continued with the attacks of the
Evangelicals on child labour, and the Benthamites on the things
which offended against the health of towns; and the phase ended
with Shaftesbury, the Evangelical, and Edwin Chadwick, the
Benthamite, working together with mutual respect and understanding on the Board of Health, with the forces of dirt, dis-
order and selfishness arrayed against them, the latter, I am afraid,
proving ultimately successful. But by the 1850s the tensions had
relaxed. John Stuart Mill had recognized some of the narrow-
ness and limitations of his father's creed, the strictest Evangeli-
canism had been remitted to the revivalist preacher, or to some
of the more fanatical parochial clergy. The old rigidities were
passing into the shadows and the thought of the third quarter
seems to be typified by that most sensible and urbane book,
Bagehot's *English Constitution*, published in 1867.

It depicts a political system in which moderation and common
sense are predominant, and Bagehot glories in them. He does
not, of course, approve of all he sees. He realizes that the landed
gentry have too much power in politics. He pours delicate scorn
on what he calls a 'deferential electorate' and he says, or makes
someone else say, of the great red-faced Tory squires who occupied so large an area of the benches of the House of Commons,
'By Jove, they are the finest brute votes in Europe!' Indeed
there was no particular reason why this professional, intellectual
society should love the powers that ruled England. They did not
share in that rule, they found it difficult even to get into the
House of Commons, and they could see the defects of their
rulers very clearly. Only ten years before Bagehot wrote, the
fate of an army perishing in a Crimean winter through sheer
official mismanagement had seemed to show up the defects of
aristocratic rule in their ugliest form. Reform was needed, but
not any reform. If the reform meant that the system of democracy was to be adopted, on the whole they did not want it.
What they did want was a society which would be more effectively controlled by educated opinion, and therefore they did not
want to see the control of society by the ugly forces which had

pulled down the railings in Hyde Park, nor by the drunken and corrupt voters who seemed to dominate so many popular constituencies. Least of all would they wish for subordination to the philistine middle class of the provinces. Of course among the professional intellectual classes there were many opinions, ranging from the radicalism of Mill to the clear reactionary creed of his friend, James Fitzjames Stephen. But I think if the professional classes had seen what a further reform of the Parliamentary system would infallibly mean, and many of them guessed it, they would by a large majority have voted against it.

If therefore the aristocracy had their hands effectively on the keys of power, if in the country there was no urgent social need for a change, if many of the most intelligent people of the country feared the surrender to democracy, why then was there a change in the direction of democracy? To answer this question it is necessary not to look at the top of society, nor at the opinions of very intelligent men in London, but to look at the foundations of the system. When one considers any political system it is necessary to ask certain questions. Upon what social structure did it rest? Where was the wealth of the community? Who were the natural élites, what are the numbers of the people who were likely to be relevant to any political problem, where did they live and in what social grouping? What were the prevalent economic relationships? The answers will necessarily affect the political conditions which prevail and probably determine the form of government of the society. It is true that a form of government may sometimes survive the social system on which it was first erected, or survive it for a period; but it is unlikely that this situation will go on indefinitely and in a society so fluid, so sensitive to change, and changing so rapidly as British society in the nineteenth century, such a survival was not likely to continue very long.

Now in the first half of the nineteenth century the old system of government had had broad social and economic foundations. The richest men in the country were still probably the great nobility. More than half of the population still lived in rural conditions, or did till after 1851, and though in the countryside the farmers were much more politically independent than they have ever been believed to be, unless they were disturbed by extremely adverse economic conditions, they were apt to vote for their landlords' candidates, while the labourers in the countryside counted not at all. The towns, it is true, were growing fast, but till some time after 1850, many of them were still by our standards quite small. They were still very often heavily influenced by a ground landlord, or a neighbouring magnate, who could control them through a local group with whom he could work. It was indeed as Bagehot said, a deferential electorate, inclined to vote for landlords or their nominees. Where it was not sufficiently deferential it was corrupt. Where a gentleman could not get in by influence, he could normally buy enough votes to get into the House of Commons.

In the third quarter these things were changing. The towns were spreading into the countryside, so that Britain was fast becoming a country with a predominantly urban population which would inevitably dictate the policy of the country. As the towns grew larger, they grew less manageable. The numbers of votes increased, probably in the end beyond the possibilities of bribery, and the law against bribery became progressively more effective. After 1868 cases of disputed elections were judged not by committees of the House of Commons, who had a certain sympathy for the way other members had got in, but by two judges in the constituency. In 1872 there was secret voting by the ballot. It did not, as is sometimes said, stop bribery, but it must have helped. In 1883 the Corrupt Practices Act was passed, and it probably did stop bribery. The old methods were passing away, and at the same time a drastic change was taking place in a good many constituencies. For a long time money had been accumulating in the hands of men who were outside the circles through which the constituency was normally controlled. The same kind of change was taking place in the country at large. The great nobility remained the richest men in the country, but other important rich men and leaders of society emerged from the new industrial system to challenge their predominance.

Moreover, the success and stability of the system which had prevailed in Britain between 1846 and 1866 had depended upon a rather delicate balance, the equal prosperity of industry and agriculture. The disturbances of the earlier part of the century had occurred partly because those two sides of national life had not been equally prosperous. Between 1813 and 1836 agriculture was in decline and as I tried to show, it was largely the discontent of the agriculturalists that upset first the old King's government before 1830, and then the Whigs between 1833 and 1841. On the other hand, between 1838 and 1843 industry and commerce were in very great difficulties, and the result was the violent attack by the Anti-Corn Law League on the laws which agriculture valued. In 1846 this phase came to an end. When Peel repealed the Corn Laws in 1846 he calculated that both agriculture and industry would enjoy equal prosperity, and, after a moment of uncertainty, so they did for more than twenty years. But the prosperity of agriculture was based on adventitious circumstances which Peel had not foreseen. It was based on the discovery of gold in California and Australia, based on the Crimean War and the Civil War of the United States, and Peel's calculation that an increasing industrial population would always mean an increasing demand for the produce of British agriculture proved to be false.

Therefore, in due course, British agriculture or large sections of British agriculture began to succumb to foreign competition, and with an enormously increased urban population, there could be no going back on the part of either party to the creed of protection to which agriculture had clung in its earlier bad period. In fact Nemesis struck after 1874. In the ensuing six years that part of agriculture that depended on the growing of wheat, especially in the heavy clay lands, suffered severely and the farmers looked up to the Tories who were in power and received no help. The Conservatives therefore began to lose county seats in the elections of 1880, a movement which was continued by the third Reform Bill of 1884, which enfranchised the agricultural labourers and culminated in the passing of a considerable amount of the countryside into radical and Liberal hands in the general election of 1885.

The old ruling class still remained extraordinarily strong, but its social and economic foundations were, from the 1860s onwards, gradually being eroded, and if they lost their power the obvious heir was the urban industrial middle class of Britain. Indeed, they already had a good deal of power in the country.

In many towns and urban areas the local leadership was gradually slipping into their hands from men who were most notable
as nominees of one of the old landowners. They already had not
a little political influence. It is true that men from the industrial
classes, if they did not have exalted connections, did not enter
cabinets or become Prime Ministers. The parties which existed
before 1867 were outside their control and the industrial population did not have its fair share of the seats in the House of
Commons. Nevertheless the members representing industrial
constituencies seem to have taken more than their share of the
time of the House. They were probably able to talk more co-
gently and at greater length than the 'finest brute votes in
Europe'. This was important. In an age when debate counted
for much and when the initiative in national affairs lay still with
the individual member, the character of a particular member
would matter a great deal more than it does now, and one member of character and ability in the House of Commons out-
weighed a good many silent ones.

Moreover the leaders of industrial towns could if they wanted
be masters in their own neighbourhood. The Municipal Reform
Act of 1835 had handed the government of towns to those who
could gain a majority in the town. It had indeed produced a
more drastic change and effected a more complete social change
in its own sphere than was effected by the Parliamentary Reform
Act of 1832. This might be more important than appears at
first sight. The actual powers granted by the Act were mean and
uninspiring, but with the possibilities of using adoptive Acts
like the Public Health Act of 1848, or of promoting private legislation social decisions of the utmost importance could be taken
by town councils. Indeed it has been said by a modern historian
that in the middle of the nineteenth century more important
work was likely to be done by members of town councils than
was likely to be done by members of the contemporary House
of Commons. And if, for instance, the importance of political
work can be established by the fact that it actually preserves
life there would appear to be truth in this. In the middle of the
century the death rate in a town depended largely on whether
it had developed a satisfactory sanitary system or not, and
whether it had done so depended largely on the quality of the

town council. In the 1840s, 1850s and 1860s a good town council might do a very great deal, and a bad one very little, with appropriate results on the local death rate. It is a little difficult to think of much that the House of Commons actually did between the repeal of the Corn Laws and the second Reform Bill that was of greater importance.

The urban middle classes were therefore very powerful in their own sphere. They did not, of course, form a completely coherent society with uniform political opinions, principles and prejudices. Most towns and urban areas contained Tories, sometimes considerable numbers of Tories. They were normally associated with the Church of England, and in many cases probably derived from the group which had governed the town before the municipality was reformed. In 1836, after the 1835 Act, they had in most cases been driven out of power, and Dissenters, or what were called 'Church Whigs', had taken their places. But they remained in existence. In some cases they formed a permanent minority in the town, at times a large one. In a few other cases they recovered power, as in Liverpool in 1841. Indeed the urban Tories in the West Riding and Lancashire played an important part in the general election of 1841. They carried some important seats, as in Leeds and Bradford and the West Riding itself—and shook the Liberals in others. In this period many of them were actively engaged in the attack on the New Poor Law, and in the fight for legislation to reduce the hours which women and children were allowed to work in factories, and this in some places brought them into alliance with another element in town life, the working class element.

As it develops, capitalism normally seems to create a fissure in society between the owners of the capital required for industrial production and the labour employed, a fissure which in the end will have political consequences. There were already signs of this fissure opening in Britain, both the movement for factory reform between 1830 and 1847 and the Chartist movement between 1838 and 1848 were symptoms of it. In the first half of the century it had not developed everywhere, for instance it was slow to appear in places like Birmingham or Sheffield where much industry was for long carried on in small concerns where the master worked alongside his hands and there was a natural union of thought and purpose. However, in Lancashire and elsewhere, where advanced manufacturing was already in evidence, this social division was already becoming important. Clearly it would in due course strike right across the urban society of Britain.

That time was, however, not yet arrived. In mid-century there was enough unity in urban society to make it formidable, and yet, in spite of its local power and growing importance, it was in a position of subordination in the state. It had already struck at the aristocratic domination of the country in the attack on the Corn Laws. Tempers had moderated since then but the aristocratic control of power could not go on forever, and the campaign against the Corn Laws seemed to suggest the lines on which the attack would be renewed. For there was one very significant fact about the Anti-Corn Law campaign—it was a religious movement. Cobden had from the start intended that it should be. He consciously modelled his agitation on the antislavery movement. He attracted leading men from the antislavery movement into it and used their techniques and, in order to emphasize the religious and moral character of the movement, he convened in 1841 a conference of seven hundred Dissenting ministers to Manchester whose task it was to declare that the Corn Laws were 'against the Law of God, anti-scriptural and anti-religious'. He did this partly because he knew the antislavery campaign had been successful, but partly because he knew that was the nerve on which to play if he was to rally the classes that he intended to rally.

It was indeed the sensitivity of this nerve that reveals more than anything else the frontier between old and new, which divided the manufacturing classes and the provincial classes of the new Britain from the older Britain of the older culture and ways of life, a Britain which included for these purposes the professional classes. Later in the century Matthew Arnold, who was without doubt a man of the professional classes, divided Britain into three, the barbarians who were the old governing class, the philistines who were the middle class, and the populace. The barbarians he reluctantly admired, the populace did not seem to count for very much, but the philistines he attacked unsparingly. They more than anyone else rejected the gifts of culture, sweetness and light. They more than anyone else turned their backs on the civilization of educated Europe and were absurdly content with third-rate provincialism. There is no doubt that much that he said was true, there is also no doubt that much that he said was harsh and unjust. It is true that much of this new Britain had lost touch with the inherited values of civilization, but they had not had much opportunity to make acquaintance with them. Many of them had risen rather rapidly from humble circumstances where educational opportunities were negligible. Even those who had started at a higher point socially may have received a meagre education. A great deal of middle class education was poor, and in many cases the demands of commerce and industry had been so urgent and had come so early in life that there had been little chance for them to go to school.

But there had always been a chapel to go to on Sundays, from which they could gain a modicum of culture, much religious instruction and a great deal of moral denunciation. So it is small wonder that their main staple in philosophy, literature and history was the Bible and their mode of thought tended to be rather narrow, possibly self-righteous, and usually rhetorical, 'mistaking', as Matthew Arnold said, 'their natural taste for bathos, for a relish of the sublime'.

That was the condition of affairs which Cobden understood, he realized that this was the kind of idea to which he should play, that a moral issue enforced by biblical illustrations was the stimulus to which the classes which he wanted to excite, would be most likely to respond. In that sign he hoped to conquer, and in that sign he did conquer, or appeared to do so, for the Corn Laws were repealed. Naturally, other moral agitations attractive to the religious middle class tried to repeat the success of the Anti-Corn Law League. There was the Peace Society in which Cobden himself was involved, the United Kingdom Alliance to promote the cause of temperance, or rather of total abstinence, and the Liberation Society, aimed at the disestablishment of the Church of England. They all failed. The Peace Society failed for a complex of reasons, but the failure of the

United Kingdom Alliance was a classical example of the weakness of this kind of pressure group operating from outside politics. The agents of the Alliance were sent out to ask a Parliamentary candidate to pledge himself to a particular policy and, if he refused, to advise his supporters to vote against him. A Conservative would never take that pledge, even if he believed in temperance, and his followers would not care about anything the Alliance might say. The Liberal, especially if he were a conscientious Liberal, might have difficulties about the pledge, and if he refused it would put his followers into an intolerable dilemma. Either they would vote against him and bring the Tory in, or they would disregard the behests of the United Kingdom Alliance. It was a device most effectively designed to embarrass friends and assist enemies.

The men who ran the Liberation Society were much more realistic and intelligent. They saw that the proper thing to do was to attack the Liberal constituency organization before the candidate was chosen, and in 1862 they started a general campaign for this purpose in England, and particularly in Wales, where the revolt of the Welsh-speaking Nonconformity against an English-speaking Established Church and squirarchy was already begun. And they were helped in their campaign by two things. In 1867—late in time, and even so taking the shape it did largely as the result of accident—there came the second Reform Bill creating a much enlarged electorate. And secondly there seemed to emerge the right man at the right moment in the right place.

Mr Gladstone seemed providentially designed to weld old powerful Whig and new moral Liberal into an effective alliance. He was a man of two tribes. He was both the associate of the barbarians and the idol of the philistines. Indeed he should have been a member of a third tribe, which might be called the pundits, because he gained a first-class at Oxford and was for long member of Parliament for Oxford. Therefore many members of the intelligent professional classes looked on him as a traitor, when he slipped and slid into popular courses. His earlier career had been that of a highly favoured aristocratic politician. He was the son of a Liverpool merchant, but went to Eton and to

Christ Church, Oxford, then the traditional schools of statesman-
ship. He entered the House of Commons almost immediately
after going down, and was trained in the business of government
by the great master of it, Sir Robert Peel. He married into the
aristocracy, for he married a Littleton, a member of a great political family. In due course he became the ally of such men as Lord
John Russell, the Duke of Argyll, and the Marquis of Hartington, to whom he was connected by marriage. These were the
people he knew and understood. His best friend in politics was
probably the Earl of Granville. He had been successful, and by
the middle 1860s he was the natural heir to the Prime Minister-
ship, under the old Whig dispensation, when at last Palmerston
consented to die and John Russell to retire. Yet he was a man
of the other tribe as well. He was a great popular orator and he
spoke in a way that was likely to attract Dissenters, for he was a
deeply religious man, and his natural excitability made him
thunder and lightning over matters of moral principle in a way
that was deeply congenial to them.

In 1867 his destiny seemed clear. He had been the hero of the
Reform Bill of 1866, and he led the Liberal party to victory in
the elections of 1868, taking as a theme the promising topic of
the disestablishment of the Irish Church. Therefore it was
natural that the Dissenters should view him as the divinely appointed leader of their party, as they looked on the election of
1868 as the beginning of its victory. The result was a dismal
disappointment. They were deceived as to their strength in the
House and in the constituencies, and they had misunderstood
Mr Gladstone as many people did from time to time.
The disestablishment of the Irish Church had been a step to the
conciliation of Ireland, it had not been a first contribution to the
policy of the Liberation Society. When the Nonconformists
moved on to the disestablishment of the English Church Mr
Gladstone opposed them, and they were beaten. Worse than this,
when the government produced its measure for creating a system for public, primary education, it permitted the survival of
the church schools, which the Dissenters greatly desired to
abolish.

In order to force the hand of the government, the Dissenters
fell back on their old expedient, the formation of another body

in imitation of the Anti-Corn Law League. This was to be the
Education League with its headquarters, not at Manchester but
at Birmingham, and it was, as all the pressure groups were, another dismal failure. The education issue did not attract enough
enthusiasm to give it force, and where it did intervene, its main
result seems to have been to spoil the chances of the Liberal
candidate. Indeed, the anger of the Dissenters contributed much
to the great Liberal defeat of 1874. But before that time one
realist had seen the lesson in the situation. Joseph Chamberlain
was a young Unitarian screw manufacturer of Birmingham,
who had been involved in the Education League, and by 1872
he realized that it was doing no good. He set to work to organize
a general political attack on the aristocracy, not on one point,
but on all.

He adopted for this purpose the local Liberal association and
used the organization of the Education League to spread his
views in the country. This produced a movement which was
powerful for two reasons. The Birmingham constituency organization was, in form, very democratic. It seemed, both in Birmingham and the places that imitated it, to replace the old oligarchical method of politics by a representative system which was
based on the votes of the humblest members of the party; but
at the same time, both in Birmingham and elsewhere, it placed
the controlling powers of the constituencies in the hands of a
group of rich men who could use the plea of democracy to consolidate their power. It therefore appealed to men who wished
to gain a better position than they possessed in the old organizations. Chamberlain made himself a missionary of the system,
urging other towns to adopt it and with the help of the officials
of the Education League weaving those that did into a new
body, the National Liberal Federation.

Then at a critical moment, when his work of organizing these
constituencies was well in progress, a new wind filled his sails,
bringing with it the old leader, Mr Gladstone, who thought he
had resigned from the leadership after his defeat in 1874. There
had been trouble among the European subjects of the Turks,
and there had been a revolt in Bulgaria which the Turks had
put down by their normal methods which were not pretty. Now
Turkey was traditionally the ally of England and we had not

troubled too much about her fashion of government. But on this occasion two things made a difference. Modern methods of reporting gave a vigorous picture in English journals of the kind of things which happened, and the fate of the eastern Christians deeply interested High Churchmen, who were becoming much interested in the Orthodox Church—these were the churchmen, Liddon, Freeman and Canon MacColl, who were most closely in touch with Mr Gladstone. They interested him in the matter, drew him out of retirement and made him raise his mighty voice against the iniquities which were taking place on the other side of Europe. First he tried to press the government to stop them, or at least to dissociate themselves from the government that was guilty of them, and then he attacked ministers, particularly Disraeli, for complicity.

The agitation of 1876 only lasted six months and failed in its object, but it probably changed the history of the country. It reunited Gladstone to the Dissenters, for they joined in the agitation, and this time the alliance was not to be dissolved. In fact, it put Gladstone at the head of Chamberlain's movement, and when in 1877 the Education League was finally turned into the National Liberal Federation, Gladstone was asked to address it, and it was clear from that moment that Gladstone was the leader of the party again. He was to all purposes leader in the election of 1880 when Gladstone's crusading, Chamberlain's organization and the Conservative failure in the countryside produced a great Liberal victory. Perhaps at long last the new Dissenting manufacturing Britain was on its way to that control of the country which it had so long felt it should by rights enjoy—perhaps. But, of course, you can never prophesy in politics.

Burn, W. L., *The Age of Equipoise*. London, 1964.
Hanham, H. J., *Elections and Party Management: Politics in the Time of Disraeli and Gladstone*. London, 1959.
Jones, W. D., *Lord Derby and Victorian Conservatism*. Oxford, 1956.
Shannon, R. T., *Gladstone and the Bulgarian Agitation 1876*. London, 1963.

Southgate, Donald, *The Passing of the Whigs, 1832-1886.* London, 1962.

Vincent, J., *Formation of the Liberal Party, 1857-1868.* London, 1966.

Williams, W. E., *The Rise of Gladstone to the Leadership of the Liberal Party, 1859 to 1868.* Cambridge, 1934.

4

THE FATE OF LIBERALISM

IT IS CLEAR that in using the phrase—'the fate of Liberalism' I might be referring to several different things. They are possibly connected and the possibility of their connection is important, but they are distinct from one another and they should be considered separately.

The first and most obvious of the things to which I might be referring is the fate of the Liberal party, triumphant in 1880, but out of office for more than half of the remaining twenty years of the century, returning to power with great force in 1905, then after 1918 relegated to the position of the least powerful of three parties, to become in due course a small remnant in the scene which it had long dominated. But there are other interpretations of the phrase. It might mean, and in the minds of many people it would naturally mean, the fate of that social and economic conception which supported the belief that the best social values could be assured by liberating them from unnecessary interference by the state or by anyone else. Thus, many people believed that trade should be freed to find its most profitable routes; that taxation should be kept down to a minimum, particularly indirect taxation, because that pressed upon the poor; that people should be encouraged to do things for themselves, partly because that encouraged self-reliance, partly because they were the best judges of what they wanted and partly also because they had an inherent right to decide things for themselves. And to this view of Liberalism, as to all views of Liberalism, should be attached these important basic principles, relating to the freedom of the individual, which had been worked out in the long story of English history: the rule of law and the protection of the individual against arbitrary treatment by the State, equality before the law, freedom of opinion, freedom of worship, and so on.

Much of that Liberal creed is out of fashion nowadays, indeed much of it could not be sustained throughout the nineteenth century. Many essential services could not be supplied by voluntary effort. It was necessary to have public elementary education, although old-fashioned Nonconformists objected to it, indeed, it was necessary to make all children go to school. It was necessary to impose on all cities and towns a minimum standard of cleanliness and hygiene. It was necessary to pass Acts to control the operation of the railways. It was necessary to pass Acts to protect children and even adults in factories. It was necessary to pass Acts to prevent the pollution of food, of rivers, and of the atmosphere. Each particular interference became cumulative, increasingly formidable and extensive, and new areas of state interference were constantly developing so that by the end of the century the age of collectivism had unavoidably succeeded the age of *laissez faire*.

In saying this it is important to remember that a modified creed of *laissez faire* had been the creed of a large number of not inhumane, not unintelligent men, and that it had in fact been a defensible creed which had done good. In 1887 came the Queen's first jubilee, and Tennyson wrote an extraordinarily gloomy poem called 'Locksley Hall—Sixty Years After'. In order to efface the impression of this poem, Mr Gladstone wrote an article in the *Nineteenth Century*, giving what he thought were the best achievements of the age. Among them he notes with approval many positive acts of state interference, including the Factory Legislation. But he reserves his greatest praise for those things which helped people to help themselves, and what he cites under that head is impressive.

Even for comparatively poor people the policy of *laissez faire* had done much. Its basic principle was perhaps the reduction of taxation. In 1842, seeing the great distress in the country, Gladstone's master, Peel, had said that what he wanted to do was to make this country a cheap country for living in, so that the poor man could at least afford his loaf of bread and the middling man his leg of mutton. Both he and his great pupil had done their best to bring this about, and the policy of cheapness had been of inestimable advantage to anyone, however poor, with money to spend. Cheap food, cheap drink, cheap clothes, cheap travel, cheap soap and in some respects, though not in all, cheap

houses, all of these things could be secured for the people of
Great Britain if only the level of taxation could be kept low.

For this reason Mr Gladstone was filled with a passion for
economy in public spending so fierce that at times he does not
seem to be entirely sane on that subject. Certainly both he and
the British Treasury, over which he so often presided, seem on
occasion to have lost all sense of proportion, all sense of
humanity and all common sense. Perhaps their finest effort in
the nineteenth century was to refuse to allow the purchase of
fodder for the baggage animals in the Crimea, because the com-
missary had only ~~requested~~, and not ~~required~~, that the fodder
be sent. Therefore they saw a way to economize and the fodder
was not sent, and the animals died, as animals do without fodder.
Partly at least as a result of this the army starved in the trenches,
but the principles of economy were preserved. However, I think
the story I like best comes from later in the century when a
great public servant, Sir Theophilus Shepstone, was trying to
persuade the Zulus not to enter the Transvaal and put the
people in the isolated farms to the assegai. At the height of that
crisis, Rider Haggard, the novelist, was sent galloping off on a
horse, into the night, to meet the Zulu king, who was dissuaded
from doing what he wanted to do. History passed on. The Transvaal was occupied by the British and the Battle of Majuba Hill
was fought and lost. The Transvaal was evacuated by the British.
Sir Theophilus came home and probably everyone forgot the incident; everyone, that is, but one implacable body, the British
Treasury. They wanted to know by what authority that horse
had been paid for. Sir Theophilus had to confess that in the
confusion of an admittedly critical moment he had not had sufficient authority to pay for the horse. He was therefore forced to
reimburse the money for the horse from his own pocket.

That spirit was, I am afraid, congenial to Mr Gladstone, but
it is to be remembered that in the period during which Mr Gladstone was economizing as fiercely and at times as ridiculously
as he did, he was not economizing on the social services, he was
economizing on the money spent on the army and navy. In
British budgets up to the end of the century the largest items
are those on military expenditure. It would be wrong therefore
to deduce from this passion for economy the conclusion that

Gladstone did not care for the social services; still less that he did not think realistically about the needs of the poor. Not only was the policy of cheapness of great importance to them, but it was accompanied by other Acts, which might be considered to come within the compass of *laissez faire,* and which were of great value to poor men, or moderately poor men. They were given the chance to save in the Post Office Savings Bank, to recover their debts reasonably easily, to co-operate for certain purposes and so on. Yet even though there was more to be said for the old policy than is normally allowed, it could not go on for ever. Not only was the development of collectivism inevitable, but the passion for economy which consumed Mr Gladstone died down, particularly after the Liberals had adopted an advanced social policy in 1906. Other Liberal policies, sound money, and even free trade, followed it out. Therefore, if by Liberalism is meant the social and economic policy of Mr Gladstone, it really went out with the nineteenth century. Possibly the last of the Liberals was that luscious autumn blossom, Sir William Vernon Harcourt; though some connoisseurs might name Campbell-Bannerman and John Morley.

However, the fate of Liberalism can mean something more serious than this. Liberalism was a peace loving creed. It depended explicitly on free discussion, the appeal to reason, free elections, the constitutional process, and abstinence from force. But from early in the twentieth century men showed a tendency to turn from these things to violence. Ulster armed to fight Home Rule and the Irish nationalists to fight Ulster. The suffragettes used violent means to draw attention to their cause. Between 1909 and 1913 there was probably more continuous and widespread industrial warfare than ever before; this was not perhaps an actual appeal to violence, but it was not an appeal to reason either. In the Balkans there was endemic violence and murder leading to war, and in 1914 came the complete breakdown of international order in Europe. Some of this violence was the natural condition of the areas where it took place, and the breakdown in 1914 was partially caused by the fact that Europe was unable to isolate it. Some of it was caused by what may be called the politics of exasperation. Up to a certain point men are prepared to be peaceful, they are prepared to compromise, they may be prepared to accept the majority decision: if driven beyond that point they may turn to violence. But something more sinister was also happening at this time. People turned to violence because they desired violence, because they thought that violence was a good thing which would purify the world from things which were choking life. Towards the end of the nineteenth century a good many people seemed to have developed a strong distaste for the comfortable compromises, the stuffy conventionalities, and, so they felt, the half-truths of nineteenth-century existence. They wanted to replace them with a way of life which would be cleaner, finer, nearer to truth, if harsher and more cruel. It was partly this element, partly this distaste for the civilization which they had inherited, which led to the great popularity of Rudyard Kipling, with his stories of soldiers, administrators and ships' engineers, living hard lives in exotic places, and with his contempt for the street-bred people, which is precisely the emotion which most appeals to street-bred people when they are suffering from claustrophobia. The same strain comes out in the very brilliant stories of H. H. Munro, who wrote under the name of Saki, *Beasts and Superbeasts, The Toys of Peace, The Unbearable Bassington* and the rest. Indeed in those stories the element of ruthlessness and cruelty is more nakedly expressed. There is the same tendency abroad. Kipling was, I believe, almost as popular in France as he was in England, and in France you have that interesting book by Georges Sorel, *Réflexions sur la Violence*, published in 1908. Sorel puts the case for revolutionary syndicalism, but as I read the book, Sorel seems to be much more interested in the antiseptic value of the general strike as an ideal of violence and a myth of violence, as opposed to what he feels to be the dishonest parliamentary socialism of a man like Jaurès. In Germany one of the compelling motives of Nietzsche was contempt for the civilization of the Germany which had come into existence after 1870, and his work was misunderstood and pushed by other Germans to crude extremes which he never intended. The same contempt for the inherited virtues of civilization was shown by another group of young people in Germany before 1914, the Wandervögel, young people who wandered about Germany, sleeping out of doors and explicitly rejecting the values of their parents and also of Christianity; and a fatigue with peace and a thirst for military glory were probably pretty strong among the crowds that cheered the German troops when they marched away in 1914.

Since 1914, and still more since 1933, the world has had its bellyful of violence, and many there are who would give everything they have to return to the creeds which appealed to a rational, civilized discussion, which stressed tolerance and were prepared to achieve settlement by compromise. But a rejection of spiritual sanctions, an increase in the politics of desperation, an increase in the rule of mankind by the means of mass hysteria, has produced a world of totalitarian States, of incessant propaganda, of slogans and of student demonstrations, in which it is not easy to get back to the old ideal. Meanwhile men and women have lost their sense of the value of that element which, as I said in my first lecture, does seem to be essential to Liberalism, the belief in the value of liberty.

Perhaps that belief starts to go as collectivism necessarily takes the place of *laissez faire*. A reasonable answer to any claim on behalf of personal liberty has been to say—'What is the value of liberty when a man is ill-educated, unhealthy and intolerably housed?' Theoretically it should be possible to renew that claim for liberty when those physical disabilities have been removed or reduced; practically such a renewal is normally useless for by that time men have learnt to obey, and the state has acquired powers which it is unwilling to surrender. Nor is it clear that the beliefs which many people entertain nowadays will either make people desire that men and women should make free choices for themselves, or sustain a claim that they have a right to do so. For if, as many believe, men and women are only complicated mechanisms set in motion by reflex actions it is difficult to see what the phrase 'to make a free choice' can possibly mean, and if the basis of philosophy is frankly materialistic, as it is for many people, then it is difficult to see that the word 'right' can imply more than convenience based on that potentially tyrannical doctrine, the greatest happiness of the greatest number. Therefore neither modern habit, nor yet modern principle, would seem to support that belief in human liberty which was deemed to be essential to the creed of Liberalism in the past.

It would be hard to say how far these ideologies affected the fortunes of the Liberal party in Britain. Probably they did assist its decline, but certainly other more mundane factors were effective in the matter. One possibility is that the decline of the Liberal party was largely caused by the disappearance of those social conditions which in the past had made it powerful. It had depended on the co-operation of rich men and poor men, of workers and men of the middle classes. Changes which had started in the late nineteenth century, but which seem to have gone forward at a much greater speed in the war years between 1914 and 1918, may have undermined this alliance in a good many constituencies. Working men may have become more class conscious, and between 1914 and 1918 more prosperous. The power of organized labour certainly increased, so that after 1918 it became to seem to be less and less necessary and less and less palatable for a working class constituency to be represented by a Liberal. Meanwhile life was becoming more secularized and Nonconformity was losing its grip on the people. How extensive a change this must have made can be seen from the number of derelict chapels in British streets, which were once the centre of life and enthusiasm, and Liberalism, and are now changed miserably into offices, small factories and warehouses.

It ought to be said, however, that the usual account of the failure of the Liberal party does not require an explanation based on any social conditions. It relates it to three factors: the split over Home Rule in 1886, the outbreak of 'imperialism' at the end of the century and the quarrel between Lloyd George and Asquith in 1918. The account normally runs as follows. The general election of 1880 seemed to promise the Liberals a prolonged lease of power. They were a divided party with the Whigs under Hartington and the Radicals under Chamberlain at loggerheads, but they were in great strength in the country and under the inspired lead of Gladstone. However, theirs was a troubled inheritance shadowed by the Transvaal, by Egypt and above all by Ireland, and it was Ireland which tore the party into two when Gladstone, after five years frustration, adopted Home Rule in 1886. This decision drove not only Hartington but also Chamberlain into opposition, and so caused the Liberal defeat of 1886, and this division over Ireland crippled the Liberal party till the end of the century. Nevertheless, in spite of it, the Liberals did regain enough unity to win the general election of 1892, and to enable Gladstone, fighting like a hero, to bring in his second Home Rule Bill, which was thrown out by the House of Lords. Gladstone was old and his colleagues timorous, and they were not prepared to appeal to the people. And so, at long last, Mr Gladstone retired, and the Liberal party fell under the extremely confusing rule of Lord Rosebery, and as a result went down into defeat in the election of 1895. The Conservatives remained in office till 1905, maintained in power partly by the divisions of the Liberals and partly by the popular appeal of 'imperialism', which reached its peak in the Boer War and the 'Khaki' election of 1900. But in 1905 they fell divided by the tariff reform urged by Joseph Chamberlain, and were severely beaten in the general election of 1906 by the reaction against protection and imperialism. The Liberals returned to office with one of the ablest governments they had ever produced, but in 1914 came the Great War and the mortal rivalry between Lloyd George and Asquith. And because Lloyd George refused to support more than half of the Liberal party in the coupon election of 1918, which the coalition won, they were pushed out of the way and Labour was given the chance of becoming the chief opposition party. And then, because a system of election which depends on single seats is always hard on third parties, the great Liberal party gradually shrank to a small faithful remnant.

No doubt there is much truth in this picture. But I am afraid much of it rests largely on speculation. It is important to realize that an account like this will have been produced even by the most reputable historians without any attempt to find out what actually happened in the various general elections. Normally they will have assumed that the result was controlled by some general cause which the general sequence of events seems to suggest as probable. This assumption is not normally tested by research in the local press, the poll-books before 1872, the reports of political agents or of the whips, or any of those who made it their business to find out what was actually happening, all of which might show something of what went on in the constituencies. Indeed such accounts are often made without the construction of lists to show what boroughs changed hands, what the voting strength of each candidate was, what boroughs were contested, and, what is very important, how large a proportion of the registered voters went to the poll.

All this constituency research is very laborious, but until it is done generalization is mere guess-work. Some of it has been done for the later nineteenth century, but it is incomplete, especially at the end, and probably I ought to stop the lecture at this point and say that I do not know enough to go further. However, I am going to risk some very tentative suggestions, or guesses.

The point at which to start seems to be the split in the Liberal party over Home Rule. This probably hit the Liberals hard in the general election of 1886, for the election came immediately after the division on the question and a great many Liberals, under the leadership of Bright and Chamberlain had voted against Gladstone, and even where the constituencies' organizations remained faithful to Gladstone there was little time to extemporize new arrangements. Such division in a party immediately before an election normally has serious results, but it does not often happen. 1886 ought therefore to be considered to be an exceptional election and taken out of the series. This is not true of either 1892 or 1895. In 1892 the Irish question was pressing, but not unduly so, and although the Liberal party was reorganized, and a certain number of the people who had deserted over Mr Gladstone in 1886 had returned, the Liberal majority was reduced from what it had been in 1885. And again in 1895 the Conservatives had a majority. There is therefore a fairly continuous decline in the Liberal vote. It would require a good deal of evidence to prove that this was primarily due to the reaction against Home Rule, especially in 1895. Certainly Home Rule had deprived the Liberals of the support of some of the Liberal Unionists. But it must be remembered that when Chamberlain went he did not carry with him the National Liberal Federation, much of which remained true to Gladstone, while the departure of the Whigs seems to have been only one phase in a general exodus of noblemen and gentlemen from the Liberal party which started as early as 1865.

Therefore it looks as if something else besides Home Rule

was causing the decline of the Liberal party in the last twenty years of the nineteenth century and as if the effect of that split had been exaggerated. If this was so, however, there ought to have been some symptoms of decline in the election of 1885, which took place before the split. This was a resounding victory for the Liberals, but it was a paradoxical victory. The Liberals lost in the towns and gained in the counties. The urban losses may have been due to Parnell's advice to the Irish to vote Tory, or to the Roman Catholic dislike of the Liberal educational policy. But if you take 1885, 1892 and 1895 together it looks as if there was some other factor gradually loosening the Liberal grip on some urban areas. What it was may be suggested by going back as far as the general election of 1868. This was a defeat for the Conservatives, but there were three significant areas which promised better things for them. There was Lancashire, where there was a good deal of popular Toryism, based partly upon the popularity of the Tory landlords like Lord Derby, partly on the intense dislike of the Irish, who were there in great numbers, and partly on the fact that workers were apt to remember that Liberals like John Bright had opposed factory reform. The second promising area was Westminster, where W. H. Smith, a convert after the death of Palmerston, beat John Stuart Mill. The third was Middlesex, where Lord George Hamilton beat Labouchère. Of these areas Middlesex promised most for the future, for Middlesex had become a suburban area, and the victory symbolized two things which were going to be important. First there was the tendency of people who had grown rather wealthy to leave the towns and live in an environment which was remote from their poorer neighbours and remote from the influences, religious, social and political, which had hitherto controlled them; and secondly there was a tendency for the same people whether they lived in suburbs or in towns to change over in politics, because they were beginning to copy the habits of the old governing classes and to come to believe that they had more to lose than to gain from Liberal reform. According to this theory, therefore, there was a constant flow of rather wealthy people from the Whigs and Liberals to the Conservatives and the creation in the suburban areas of what were in effect single-class communities which made admirably safe Tory seats. It is this process, it is argued, which partially accounts for the constant increase of Conservative strength from 1885 up to and probably including 1900.

A certain amount of work has been done to confirm this theory, but the work is not easy. It is not for one thing, easy to determine what Parliamentary divisions should be considered to be suburban. Something can be done using rateable values, the location of industries, the closeness of settlement in particular areas; but the results are often inconclusive and the social structure of any particular area often changes continuously. More than this the social elements which control a constituency probably change with the size of the poll in any election. If fewer people vote, the control may be middle class; if more, working class. Indeed this may in part explain what happened at the end of the century. The Liberals did not offer enough to make enough working people bother to vote, but in 1906 both Liberals and Labour made a more positive bid for the working class vote and the Tories were swamped.

It is not easy to say as yet in what ways the election of 1900 differs from that of 1906. It is not really known how far 1900 was affected by nationalist feelings excited by the Boer War, or how far it was simply a repetition of what had happened before. It seems clear, however, that 1906 should be considered to be an exceptional election for the same reason that 1886 must be considered to be exceptional. Immediately before the election the Conservatives had been divided, they were in some confusion and their party machine was not working well. The two elections of 1910 are probably a better guide to their normal strength. Indeed they seemed to be increasing in power at the expense of the Liberals between 1914 and 1918. Certainly the most recent work seems to show that what happened in 1918 was not that Lloyd George threw a large number of Liberals to the wolves by not giving them a coupon—a recommendation signed by himself and the Conservative leader, Bonar Law—but that he managed by agreement with Bonar Law to save a certain number of Liberals who would have otherwise lost their seats.

Meanwhile something else was happening which permanently affected both parties and removed certain constituencies from them. This was the emergence of the Labour party. The steps which led to the formation of the Labour party are beyond the scope of these lectures. But it is worth-while suggesting here that in Britain, before a party becomes an effective contestant for power, it must have a reasonably reliable control in all but the most exceptional conditions of a certain basic number of Parliamentary seats. This meant not only a series of victories in marginal seats but probably that certain seats which had been reliably Conservative or reliably Liberal had to become reasonably safe for Labour, which meant in its turn, in some cases, a change in long established voting habits. It seems possible that this was happening in several constituencies between 1900 and 1922. Why it happened must as yet be a matter of speculation. It may have resulted from the decline in the power of the chapel though it is by no means certain. After all the chapel could go Labour and in any case such a change would not affect Conservative working class constituencies in Lancashire, for example. It may have been helped by a change in industry in particular constituencies, or it may have resulted from the development of more militant Trade Unions, or a growth of working class self-consciousness and a realization of the possibilities of more purely working class leadership. It was probably assisted by the conditions that prevailed in the war of 1914-18, with an increase in working class prosperity and an increase in the number of Trade Union members. But if such a change happened in a sufficient number of constituencies it would hit both the Conservative and the Liberal parties, and make a more or less permanent change in their size, and, if not at first, then at least ultimately it would do the Liberals most harm.

All this is, however, based on conjecture and, what is more, conjecture which extends beyond my scope. It should suffice for my purposes to say that after 1886 the Liberals seem to have lost ground to the Conservatives, that their victory in 1906, so long delayed by the power of the old aristocratic classes, lasted for a very brief period, and that after 1900 a new age seems to start in which the old Liberalism seems to be outdated, and after a brief revival the old party has to give way to Labour. Future research in the constituencies may tell us why this change in parties took place, but as far as I am concerned, I have come to the end of my beat and next time will turn to the problem of 'imperialism' which will take me back to the beginning of the century.

Dangerfield, George, *The Strange Death of Liberal England.* London, 1936 (also in paperback).

Ensor, R. C. K., *England 1870-1914.* Oxford, 1936.

Garvin, J. L. and Amery, J., *The Life of Joseph Chamberlain.* Vols 1-3, London, 1932-51.

Hammond, J. L. and Foot, M., *Gladstone and the Irish Nation.* London, 1938, 1964.

Norman, E. R., *The Catholic Church and Ireland in the Age of Rebellion, 1859-1873.* London, 1965.

O'Brien, C. C., *Parnell and his Party, 1880-1890.* Oxford, 1957.

Sorel, Georges, *Reflections on Violence,* translated with an introduction by T. E. Hulme. First publ. London, 1916.

Wilson, Trevor, *Downfall of the Liberal Party, 1914-1935.* London, 1966.

5

IMPERIALISM

I WISH TO TURN BACK from the problems which the expansive forces of the nineteenth century created within Britain to some of the problems they created outside Europe. I wish, however, to discuss these problems as they are suggested by a question of semantics.

In his *Sesame and Lilies* John Ruskin has an interesting passage in which he discusses what he calls 'masked words'. These are words with strong emotive force but with equivocal meanings, or no meaning at all, which men and women use to hide their prejudices and enforce their arguments. The use of such words has not ceased since his day: indeed the development of a quasi-scientific style in public discussion has secured that their use should be more frequent and more deadly. For a word can be given every appearance of exact meaning, as if the application of such a word was the result of careful and objective scientific analysis while in fact it is simply part of the routine name-calling, common to all political controversies, national or international. In fact in the quite recent past the meaning and implications of the word may have changed from time to time as circumstances changed.

It would be interesting to make a list of such words in common use at the moment. The language of abnormal psychology has supplied some very valuable ones; so has the language of economic analysis and political science. The words 'socialism', 'communism', 'capitalism' or 'exploitation' can all be used with suitably varying meanings and the right appearance of exactitude, and they can all be used to excite a man's passions and mask his presuppositions. However, the word which is probably in most general use at the moment is the word 'imperialism'. It has in fact been recently so generally employed that its mask is becoming a little thin and the prejudice behind it rather obvious. For its use has become unashamedly selective. 'Imperialism' is now very largely what another nation has done or is

61

doing. Your own interventions in the affairs of other nations by means of trade, propaganda, diplomatic action or armed invasion are more likely to be the result of conscientious anti-imperialism. Where you invade you will 'liberate', even if the people so invaded may desperately resist your incursion and may not in many cases actually survive it for very long.

The word has a suitably varied and ambiguous history. The modern use of it derives mainly from the writings of Lenin, endorsed by a good deal that has been written and felt in the United States. Lenin seems to have depended largely on the book of an Englishman, J. A. Hobson. This was a polemical tract against the kind of activity which Hobson held had led to the South African war. For a work of contemporary controversy Hobson's *Imperialism* is a serious and intelligent piece of work, but it would not now be considered by students of the subject to be a decisive analysis of a difficult and complicated problem, and clearly his general conclusions ought not now to be used without a careful consideration of the important and varied literature which has been produced on the subject since he wrote.

If you go back before Hobson you will find that the word bore at different times very different meanings. In fact it could be used in ways that had no relation to overseas possessions at all. For instance in 1857 Charles Kingsley wrote:

Tired of the helplessness of *laissez faire* educated men are revolting fast to Imperialism; and when once the commercial classes shall have discovered, as France has already done, that a Despotism need not interfere in any wise with the selfish state of society, but that [and here he mentions two firms] can make money as fast under Napoleon as under Christ, Manchester will not lift a finger to save the liberties of England.

In this extract 'imperialism' relates to the Third Empire and so to the kind of dictatorial régime that Napoleon had set up in France. But as G. M. Young noted in his portrait of the Victorian Age, the word 'empire' could also be simply used as a synonym for 'realm' or 'kingdom'. It could be said that such and such city was the worst or the best drained city 'in the empire', meaning simply in England or Britain. This was a usage which had some theoretical and historical justification. In 1532 Henry

VIII's Act of Appeals declared that this realm of England was an 'Empire', or as he wrote it 'Impire'. He meant by this that it was an autonomous and sovereign State, his object being to prevent Catherine of Aragon from appealing to Rome against the annulment of her marriage in England. This definition of the meaning of the word survived into the eighteenth century. In his commentaries on the laws of England published in 1765 Blackstone wrote as follows:

The meaning therefore of the legislature, when it uses these terms of *empire* and *imperial,* and applies them to the realm and crown of England, is only to assert that our king is equally sovereign and independent within these his dominions, as any emperor is in his empire; and owes no kind of subjection to any other potentate upon earth.

On the other hand in the eighteenth century the word 'empire' seems to have been also used with special reference to overseas dominion. It was presumably so used by Burke in 1775 in his great speech on the conciliation of the American colonies, where he says that the participation of freedom was the 'sole bond, which originally made and must still preserve the unity of the Empire'. It was so used by Adam Smith in the *Wealth of Nations* published in the following year. When discussing colonies he says: 'To found a great Empire for the sole purpose of raising up a people of customers may at first sight appear as a project fit only for a nation of shopkeepers.' And he goes on to imply that if they did this they would be pretty foolish shopkeepers. This passage, which criticized the old motives for empire building, was naturally well known to the free trade writers of the nineteenth century. It is quoted in a longish extract in Porter's *Progress of the Nation,* a standard book of reference of the middle of the nineteenth century. Porter himself restricted the word 'Empire' to the Indian Empire, possibly because that was under the same kind of dictatorial rule as had come to exist in France. Elsewhere he was inclined to talk about 'the Colonies', and in one place he remarked that colonies of settlement are the only ones which are properly called colonies. Of these he approved, for though he warmly supported Adam Smith's strictures on the old colonial system he saw an advantage in retaining colonies which make it possible for what he called 'our additional numbers' to emigrate and yet not forfeit their privileges as citizens.

In this idea he reflected the thought of the radical colonial reformers, Molesworth, Wakefield, Charles Buller and the Earl of Durham, and though it is just possible that there might have been a distinction in Porter's mind between what was 'imperial' and what was 'colonial', these reformers developed a technical use of the word 'imperial' which was applied to the colonies and which was of the greatest use in the development of colonial self-government. It was foreshadowed in the Durham Report when it was suggested that all matters which concerned the colonies should be placed in the hands of the inhabitants of the colonies except those which directly concerned the Imperial government. These reserved subjects were—the form of government the colony was to have, the regulation of foreign relations and of trade with the mother country, other colonies and foreign nations, and the disposal of public lands—the last subject being important because upon it might depend the possibility of future immigration into the colony. As colonial self-government developed in the nineteenth century, this list was progressively reduced. But the conception survived that the word 'imperial' related to what concerned the empire as a whole and was still controlled by the ministry and Parliament at Westminster and distinguished from the domestic affairs of the colony, which were controlled by the colony itself. This distinction is reflected in the description in Australia of British soldiers as 'imperials', or in the name of the force which Australia sent overseas in the 1914-18 war, which was the A.I.F., the Australian Imperial Force, that is, a force of Australians officered by Australians but serving under British generals in a war which had been declared on the advice of the British Cabinet.

There was a significant adaptation of this line of thought in South Africa fairly late in the nineteenth century. In 1884 Cecil Rhodes told the Cape Parliament: 'We must not have the Imperial factor in Bechuanaland.' Here also, the 'Imperial factor' he was talking about was the power of the Home government, in this case the power of the colonial office, its servants and the armed forces it commanded. Rhodes confronted this element in Bechuanaland, where it intruded itself to protect the Bechuanaland people from Boer incursions, and also in the person of Sir Harry Johnston in Nyasaland, and he became extremely anxious to keep it out of the territories he occupied in his drive north. He objected to the 'imperial factor' because it was dilatory, because it did not support his schemes for a united South Africa, because it was inclined in the interests of peace to make compromises with other European powers and also probably because it did not let him have a free hand in his native policy.

In talking of Rhodes I have, however, gone forward too fast in the history of the words 'empire' and 'imperial' in the nineteenth century. An important change in the colour and meaning of these words seems to start round about 1870. Before that time the 'Empire' had been the relatively neutral name of the territories governed by the British Crown. It was also used for authoritarian governments, in the ancient world, like the Empire of Rome, and in more modern times for the Empires of Napoleon I and Napoleon III. This use had given a special meaning to the word 'imperialism', and may have coloured the use of the word 'Empire' when applied to the British Empire, though this is doubtful. The word 'imperial' also acquired a technical meaning as characterizing matters affecting the Empire as a whole rather than a particular part of it. This, however, probably did not much concern ordinary people. In fact before 1870 ordinary people probably did not bother themselves much with the Empire as a whole. After that time more and more people in Britain seem to have become aware of the Empire as an entity, possibly as a source of problems, possibly a source of pride. As a result the words 'Empire', 'imperial' and so 'imperialism' began to assume a deeper moral significance and a greater emotive force, both attractive and repellent.

An early symptom of this change may be Disraeli's speech in the Crystal Palace in 1872 followed up by Lord Lytton's proclamation of the Queen as Empress of India in 1877, but I believe the decisive factor in the precipitation of emotion came from the other side, in 1876. In that year Gladstone took the lead in the agitation against the atrocities which the Turks had inflicted on the Bulgarians. This was not at first intended to be a party move; but it was intended to make the Conservative government stop the atrocities or at least to dissociate themselves from the Turks; when, however, they were irresponsive it turned into a general condemnation of them and in particular of the man at the head of the government, Benjamin Disraeli, now Lord Beaconsfield, whom Gladstone came to see as being in some dark way closely associated with the author of all evil. The subsequent behaviour of Beaconsfield's government, the entry of the fleet into the Bosphorus, the occupation of Cyprus, the war in Afghanistan, the Zulu war, the occupation of the Transvaal, all confirmed this impression and in 1879 in his Midlothian campaign he made a general onslaught on what seemed to him to have been a cynical policy of bullying and bluster, the wanton invasion of other people's territory and a gamble with the possibility of a European war.

Gladstone's attack was launched at a particular government at a particular moment. It was a partisan attack based on views distorted by party feeling. Gladstone was by no means just to all the people he criticized. He found it too easy to make generalizations about a variety of situations which were in fact inherently different from one another. Nevertheless his attack was an important expression of principle. It was not an attack on the British Empire as it then existed. He bitterly criticized those who would add to British responsibilities when, 'we have', already 'undertaken to settle the affairs of about a fourth of the entire human race scattered over all the world'; but he was prepared to accept existing responsibilities. What he did attack were those who would expand the Empire by force, thereby violating the right to freedom and independence of the nations or tribes whose territories were invaded. To these actions Gladstone opposed the ideal of a 'sisterhood of nations, equal, independent, each of them built up under that legitimate defence which public law affords to every nation, living within its own borders, and seeking to perform its own affairs'. That conception contains a most important principle—the principle that it is ultimately the right of every human group to live its own life and to decide its own destiny. It was, no doubt, not easy to maintain that principle; nor was it being at that moment as wantonly violated as Gladstone permitted himself to believe. Nevertheless it was an aspiration which even the most responsible statesmen and the most conscientious civil servants, however anxiously devoted to the people in their charge, frequently found difficult to appreciate. Gladstone's intuitive recognition of the importance of this principle might have been of the greatest value to the British Empire when public opinion in dependent territories began to ripen into nationalism. But unfortunately Gladstone's views were immediately caught up in to the vortex of party warfare, and his policies were overtaken by circumstances. The potentially valuable policies which his government put in hand —the conciliation of the Boers in the Transvaal, the promise of Lord Ripon's viceroyalty in India, Home Rule for Ireland—all came to nothing; while Gladstone contrived to excite an animosity against himself which was so great that anything he said or suggested was likely to be rejected with anger by a large section of the nation. The British Empire was to pay dearly for this failure.

Nemesis soon overtook Gladstone himself. His attack on Lord Beaconsfield had been dangerously mistaken on one point. For he had attributed to Beaconsfield greater clarity of intention and consistency of policy than was likely to be the explanation of the actions of that old opportunist and phrase-maker, and he had heavily underestimated the extent to which a Prime Minister is at the mercy of circumstances and not his own master. The sequel is one of the most curious ironies of history. When Gladstone came into office in 1880 he, too, was to be at the mercy of circumstances. The confused situation in the Transvaal and the hesitations of the government led to the unnecessary and disastrous campaign which ended at Majuba Hill. The crisis in Egypt led Gladstone to sanction first what he called the 'solemn and painful act' of bombarding Alexandria, and then the military invasion and occupation of the country, steps which many people have held to have been the beginning of the new imperialism. Circumstances in Central Asia in 1885 led to the incident of Penjdeh, when he allowed his government to put up a bluff, which might easily have involved Britain and Russia in war. It is possible that in each of these what Gladstone did, or assented to, was justified, but it is not difficult to conceive what he would have said about them, if they had happened while Lord Beaconsfield was Prime Minister.

Gladstone's inconsistencies are, however, of less historic importance than the political tradition to which he gave both his name and the life that sprang from the dynamic power of his personality. It was not in reality a new tradition. Even in the days of the Anti-Corn Law League there had been a good many people who deplored military adventure and looked askance at overseas colonies and dominions. Their feelings resulted from a curious mixture of genuine high principles and strictly utilitarian calculations. They had inherited from the eighteenth century the traditions that standing armies existed and wars were fought for the glory, pleasure and profit of the aristocracies of the world, and that colonial establishments were largely maintained as a comfortable resting place for the well connected. To these traditions they added a perfectly genuine Christian hatred of war, as consistently maintained as that feeling is normally maintained, and a deep distaste for those whom they suspected of delighting in the excitements and glories of the battlefield enjoyed at second hand in the newspapers. They were also convinced that wars and empires were bad business. They were expensive, they impeded commerce, since it had been proved long ago that colonies and empires were only an encumbrance to a commerce that could be carried everywhere on the peaceful wings of free trade. It would, said they, be a happy day for Britain when she owned not a yard of the soil of Asia.

The natural exponents of this creed were the Nonconformists and manufacturers who supported the Anti-Corn Law League. Cobden and Bright indeed upheld the creed throughout the middle of the century. It would be a little difficult to guess how much support they had in the country. Their opposition to the Crimean War was a complete failure and in 1857, when their natural opponent Palmerston appealed to the country over his Chinese policy he won his majority and Cobden, Bright and Milner Gibson all lost their seats. There may, however, have been contingent reasons for this disaster, and in any case it seems probable that the advance of Nonconformity in the next twenty years, and electoral reform in 1867, had greatly increased the number of supporters of this point of view by 1876, when Gladstone began his crusade. That crusade appealed to all their deepest instincts. A voice, as from Sinai, revealed to them terrible human suffering inflicted by the unspeakable Turk and wantonly disregarded to suit the uses of aristocratic and worldly diplomacy and the negligent cynicism of the man who had stepped into the shoes of Palmerston. Small wonder they responded warmly to Gladstone, small wonder they accepted his condemnation of Disraeli and his definition of Disraeli's sin. It matters little whether Gladstone was always just in what he said or consistent in what he did. In his person he consolidated a creed and in doing so he defined the enemy and gave what had to be fought a name. What he had done survived him. Nine days after his death, on the 28th of May 1898, the *Daily News* spoke of 'that odious system of bluster and swagger and might against right on which Lord Beaconsfield and his colleagues bestowed the tawdry nickname of Imperialism'.

Whether in fact the members of Lord Beaconsfield's government had made much use of that word, or if they had done so whether they would have meant what the writer of this article meant by it are perhaps points of little importance. What is important is that on the eve of the twentieth century the word had acquired a particular meaning and had become the name for a definable evil. However, by that time others had developed a very different view of what was implied by imperialism. Many people had been brought up to admire the soldiers, explorers and administrators, who had served the Empire and as they thought the peoples of the Empire. They were antagonized by people who 'preached them down', as they were also antagonized by what seemed to them the evasion of realities and self-assured righteousness of Gladstone and his followers. They had been made angry by the delays and apparent equivocations that had preceded the death of Gordon: and moreover, a positive side to imperialism had developed. A literature had grown up which seemed to point to an important ideal to be achieved through the Empire. They were Dilke's *Greater Britain*, Froude's *Oceana* and Seeley's *Expansion of England*. Above all there was Kipling with his vivid stories of men doing self-sacrificing service in harsh conditions in India. A good many hopes, romanticisms and aspirations had got caught up in the conception of Empire so that there were many who saw the Empire, and the actions which had brought the Empire into being, not as matters for shame but as things of which to be proud. There might have been excesses, but much good had been done both for England and humanity, and surely it was possible to discriminate between 'good imperialism' and 'bad imperialism'. In May 1899, therefore, the word was defined by Lord Rosebery thus: 'I mean the greater pride in the Empire which is called Imperialism. Sane Imperialism, as distinguished from what I might call wild cat Imperialism, is nothing but this, a larger patriotism.'

By the end of the century then, the evolution of the word was nearly complete. A conception had been formulated which was essentially different from those contained in the older meanings of the word, the general bearing of which was understood by most contemporaries. It was a conception which excited the most bitter disagreement. On one side of the quarrel it presented to intelligent men of high principle, both Conservative and Liberal, a defensible ideal, if to others on that side it could be made the excuse for language and actions which at best were foolish and could be worse than foolish. To the other side it presented tendencies and practices which many men very reasonably felt that it was their duty to oppose with all that they had in them, and on the same side there was much ignorant and unjust prejudice, much undiscriminating emotion. How effectively that emotion could upset the balance of a normally very civilized man can be seen in the nature of the pictures and parodies of Kipling in the otherwise very urbane writings and caricatures of Max Beerbohm, particularly perhaps in the pictures which he drew privately for his own delectation.

A word, which has been projected into the centre of the stream of politics, which has been a coin in such bitter exchanges and charged with such conflicting emotions, is likely to retain considerable emotive force. It will keep its heat; but its meaning may well change as the historical scene changes, and British history was going to effect another development in the history of the word imperialism before it passed into international currency. At the end of the nineteenth century came the South African war. This was the climax of the activities of one form of imperialism and the occasion for the rallying of the anti-imperialist forces, who indeed won their great victory in 1906. But the attack of those forces had changed ground a little. Cobden and Bright attacked in Palmerston, and Gladstone had attacked in Beaconsfield, what seemed to them to be a bullying ruthless foreign policy geared to a flamboyant and arrogant patriotism. Possibly if one had asked Cobden where the forces of commerce stood in the matter he would have said they were on his side and on the side of peace. The old Adam seemed certainly to have reappeared in Chamberlain's attack on the Boer republics, but behind him there was believed to be another sinister force, the activities of speculative finance—of the millionaires in the Rand and of the kind of forces in the city of London which Hilaire Belloc describes in his novel *Emmanuel Burden*. It was this belief which led to the writing of Hobson's *Imperialism*, the conclusions of which Lenin generalized to cover all the relations between European nations and their colonies, in a way that Hobson had not intended.

So far I have been writing about words, now I wish to turn to the things which the words purported to describe and the best way to start doing this seems to be to drop out of the discussion, at least for the moment, the emotive words 'imperialism' and 'empire', and to begin with what seems to be an unassailable fact. In the conditions of the nineteenth century it was inevitable that the Western European nations should expand into the rest of the world, and among the Western European nations I must include the citizens of the United States. Western European civilization was both ebullient and self-confident, and the circumstances of Western European nations made expansion to be, sometimes a necessity, sometimes a much desired luxury. Overcrowded population needed new places for settlement, the expanding industry of the industrial revolution needed markets and raw materials. Moreover struggles between European States sometimes seemed to require control of strategical areas outside Europe, while the desire for prestige sometimes led governments to occupy territories which had no strategic, or any other, value.

Apart from the obstacles presented by unexplored territories, by physical difficulties such as deserts and mountain ranges, or by the impact of disease, the only possible factor which was likely to restrict these nations from satisfying their desire for expansion was rivalry among themselves. Their technology was infinitely superior to anything to be found outside Europe, or European settled countries, and with their technology went irresistible military power. In addition to that power some terrible unseen forces fought on their side: influenza, measles, smallpox, syphilis and trade spirits. These could be counted upon to clear the ground before them. For the moment, therefore, the rest of the world was at their mercy. This could lead to a morally dangerous situation, for it could lead to a belief that men from outside Europe were inherently inferior to the white men of Europe and of the United States. There was no need to consider their values, they must be subordinated to the white man's purposes.

The danger of this situation was not necessarily eliminated by the fact that those purposes were often morally defensible and sometimes inspired by the most exalted motives. The movement of migrants into unsettled areas overseas was part of the movement of men and women from the overcrowded streets and countrysides of Europe, a movement which offered the best hope of happiness to the increasing millions of the miserable and unfortunate. Much European expansion was launched by Christian missionaries. Some British expansion resulted directly from the war against slavery. A British squadron was first stationed on the West Coast of Africa to catch the slavers on that side and the West Coast settlements were formed; then a squadron was placed on the East Coast of Africa in a campaign which led to the occupation of Zanzibar and the drive towards the Great Lakes in Central Africa. Missions and the attack on slavery were inspired by religious motives, but even Americans and Europeans who were not particularly religious were apt to believe that what they had to offer was better than anything to be found outside their culture, and they could do nothing better for non-Europeans than to bring them into its ambit.

This belief, in large part, inspired Dalhousie, one of the greatest viceroys in the expansion of British India, and the mutiny which followed was, in large part, the violent reaction of an old culture threatened by a new. That reaction was understandable, but the belief that Western civilization had something of peculiar value to offer to the rest of the world was at that moment reasonable; in fact the rest of the world has now acknowledged this by making that Western civilization its own. This is no excuse for Western pride. These things are partly the result of historical accident. This situation merely meant that Western countries were, at the moment, the heirs of what was, in some respects the highest cultural tradition in the world, a tradition which they did not originate but which originated in Asia.

Even for the extension of trade there could be genuinely exalted motives. People felt that by introducing trade into undeveloped countries they offered the peoples of the world their best chance to escape from poverty and superstition and age-old oppression. For instance, Lord Salisbury claimed that the development of railways in India—would 'enable us to propagate our civilization in the most peaceful and harmless way'. It was the considered opinion of many of the most intelligent people engaged in the war against slavery in Africa that the best method of attack was to extend ordinary commerce as an alternative to the slave-trade. It was this strategy which inspired the ill-fated Niger expedition in 1841, which was intended to extend commerce as an antidote to slavery but was completely defeated by fever. The idea commended itself to Livingstone, who believed that the introduction of commerce and Christianity ('the flag following the Cross') was the best remedy for that part of Central Africa which was being desolated by slave raids. The phrase is often used satirically with the suggestion that it means that Christianity is being used merely as a mask for commerce. That is not I think necessarily true. Certainly Livingstone should be above suspicion: it is also probable that his opinion was justified by the facts.

Yet even though there might be the most genuinely good intentions on the European side, the European need to expand, and power to expand, inevitably produced at best a series of heart-breaking problems based on a series of moral equations to which no satisfactory solutions are readily available: nor are they really made more soluble by a general abuse of settlers, or squatters, or merchants, or the British government, or European nations, or the American people, nor yet by bringing into service the normal masked words—Imperialism, colonialism and exploitation.

How can one equate the needs of myriads of potential settlers of European stock with the rights of a relatively small number of primitive people living in accordance with a cultural pattern which they had established over many centuries in a country which for uncounted years they had regarded as their own? For the European settler the opening up of new lands might mean life and hope which he could get nowhere else. For the people already in those lands, be they Australian or Tasmanian or American, it probably meant death, death from the white man's weapons, or his drink or his diseases, or the disappearance of their hunting grounds, or simply from a broken heart, because the world they understood had been ruthlessly destroyed. Yet, even with the knowledge that such tragedies were by all human calculations inevitable, is it still necessary to ask the question whether those lands should not have been opened up?

Or how can one equate the traditional values of ancient civilizations such as the Indian or the Chinese with the new values which the arms and commerce of the Western nations were going to thrust upon them? It is true that those ancient civilizations often had objectionable characteristics to which the new values were antidotes. But the civilization of the West also had objectionable characteristics which might take their place. It is true that an ancient civilization might have become stagnant, yet it might be also true that no one under its influence might have desired change. The actual process of change might be infinitely damaging, it might have been effected with very mixed motives, sinister forces might easily have got out of hand. The new civilization might provoke natural resistance which would lead to a conflict such as the Indian Mutiny, and would leave memories and tensions behind and continue for long to darken race relations. Yet taking all these things into account the question must still be asked whether it would have been desirable for those ancient races and cultures to have been left undisturbed and isolated. Would it have been possible in nineteenth-century conditions?

Or to take another series of problems, supposing development was desirable, and it is difficult to decide that it was not, what ought it to have cost in immediate outlay, or in the future payment of interest or European salaries, to the country to be developed? For instance, how is one to decide how much a railway built with great difficulty through unknown country in unprecedented circumstances ought to have cost the country which it was to serve? It is, in fact, impossible to decide. Of course where there was a careless government and a great deal of corruption any development, or even imaginary development, might cost far more than the country could afford. Such a country might be left, as was Egypt, the prey of foreign bondholders. That was the misfortune that affected particular localities, just as in other parts of the world the contractor lost all his money and the country in which he worked retained the value of what he had done. Yet even leaving these misfortunes out of account one is still left with four propositions: in many cases economic development was socially desirable, in all cases economic development would cost money, in many cases the burden of that cost would come heavily on the country which had been developed, and in almost all cases it would be resented as soon as men had come to take for granted the benefits which might have been received.

I will not say that these issues were constantly before the minds of those who had to make the critical decisions of the century. Even men of undoubted good will were, often enough, not likely to see the issues involved as clearly as we can see them. Nowadays we have learnt from anthropologists much of what can be said in explanation, and perhaps in commendation, of primitive cultures; during the greater part of the nineteenth century most men did not have that knowledge. What was strange seemed too often to be degrading and contemptible, something to be altered at all costs, and the very motives which made men go out to try to help people were apt in themselves to remove from their minds any doubts about the value of what they were doing, or about the way in which they were doing it.

Take Christianity, for instance: no person not hopelessly prejudiced would deny the great value of the work done by Christian missionaries. But, like Islam or Judaism, Christianity is apt to be an exclusive creed, that is, its adherents are inclined, not only to believe that their faith is right, but that other religions are wrong, that they spring from the darkness of the human mind, and the truth is not in them. 'What though the spicy breezes blow soft o'er Ceylon's isle, though every prospect pleases and only man is vile.' Of course, the word vile can be explained. The inhabitants of Ceylon, or Java, which was the island in an alternative version, were only technically vile, theologically vile—indeed vile was possibly put in only to rhyme with isle. They were dear good fellows really and if they were vile it was not their fault. But I am afraid those words do suggest an attitude not uncommon among nineteenth-century Christians who were apt to dismiss as equally pagan any non-Christian creed, be it the most spiritual Buddhism or Hinduism, or the most austere Mahomedanism, or the most primitive and ferocious ju-ju or fetish worship. They were all 'heathens' who in their 'blindness' bowed down 'to wood or stone'.

These limitations were, however, not confined to enthusiastic Christians. Modern enlightened and advanced opinion is also apt to be an exclusive creed. It is likely to have its intelligence restricted by its sense of its own virtues and so be prevented from understanding what might be said for the institutions it attacked, or was anxious to reform.

Therefore, with the best will in the world, a man might not be able to see the value of what he menaced or was likely to destroy, and without the best will in the world he might not care. When other matters pressed it was very easy for the ordinary man of moderate good will to write off the rights and feelings of non-European races as of secondary importance. The settler fighting hard to establish himself, the merchant struggling to get trade or the soldier preoccupied in difficult and dangerous circumstances with military routine, might become at the least very cavalier in their treatment of native inhabitants who got in their way. Nor were these the worst people who might be involved. There were also slave-traders and owners, or blackbirders, or men who abused indentured or forced labour, or financiers who did not mind what havoc they caused, or the weight of the tribute they exacted. Therefore many of these moral equations might be decided arbitrarily, probably against the best interests, certainly against the wishes, of non-European peoples, and though the expansion of Europe might bring immediate protection and enfranchisement to some, and to very many more the ultimate chance of progress, to others it might bring destruction, or if not destruction the confiscation of their lands, or forced or underpaid labour, or possibly the sacrifice of the things they held sacred and, what was worst of all, continual thoughtless and ignorant contempt.

The expansion of Europe, therefore, forms an important chapter in history both bitter and hopeful. Its motives, its course and its results require careful study, but how much of the process of expansion can be satisfactorily attributed to what can reasonably be called 'imperialism'? It is true that for some of the most violent episodes in the history of expansion empires have been responsible. Imperialists invaded territory like Afghanistan because it seemed strategically necessary for them to be controlled, they used force to subjugate independent peoples and claimed that they had a 'civilizing mission' which gave them a right to do so. But such actions as these have not been confined to States which were technically called 'empires'. Other States than empires both in the nineteenth and twentieth centuries have taken control of neighbouring territory because it was convenient to them. Other States than empires have derived from the universal validity of their own scale of values a sovereign right to control the destiny of others. If the history of expansion is to be studied in its entirety it should include the development by the United States of the doctrine of 'manifest destiny', and the war with Mexico. It should include the manoeuvres by which Theodore Roosevelt prepared to secure the lease of territory which made the Panama Canal possible. In more recent times it should include such things as the Russian invasion of Poland, as the sequel of their pact with Hitler, or the Russian occupation of the independent Baltic States, Latvia, Estonia and Lithuania. It should include such matters as the Chinese occupation of Tibet. If the use of the word 'imperialism' excludes such actions as these from the discussion because they were not perpetrated by empires then it can only be said to darken counsel, because it makes it difficult to compare the obviously comparable.

And there is another difficulty. It may not seem right to categorize much nineteenth-century European expansion as 'imperialism', because it neither needed the might of empire to facilitate it, nor did it result in the extension of imperial rule. This is true of much economic expansion. There is a contrast here with the situation before the nineteenth century started. Then the object of an empire was what Adam Smith had attacked, the creation of a closed area for the trade of the home country. The colony should produce such raw materials as the home country lacked and provide customers for its manufacturers. In the nineteenth century, however, as far as Britain was concerned, this policy was replaced by the policy of free trade with all the world: the last of the old colonial system disappeared when the Navigation Acts were repealed in 1849. Certainly in British hands at that moment the policy of free trade was an aggressive policy. Goods were intruded into another country in a way that might affect that country's way of life and make things difficult for the native manufacturer. An economic pattern, which suited Great Britain, might in fact be imposed on another country. But the weapon to be used to do this was not force of arms, or the extension of territorial sovereignty; it was the much more subtle weapon of cheapness, the cheapness of the goods produced in Great Britain, a weapon which did not need the might of empire to back it up.

There were indeed exceptional cases in which force had to be used. There were areas such as China and Japan which were not prepared to receive Western trade, or only to receive it on conditions that British statesmen considered to be unsatisfactory. In such cases force was used to open the doors to Western trade, a policy which led to the British wars in China, wars in which other nations sometimes co-operated and from which other nations, including the United States, benefited as well as Britain. The process of expansion might supply other occasions for the use of force, individuals living in weak or disturbed countries might claim protection as in the notorious case of Don Pacifico, or debts might need to be collected, or the rights of creditors safeguarded as in the case of Egypt. The readiness with which statesmen sometimes resorted to the argument of force in these quarrels was the unfortunate result of the great disparity between the strength of the major European powers and the rest of the world. But these occasions were only the contingent consequences of the movement caused by the ebullient power of a world-wide commerce, which normally did not need the power of empire to secure its entry, and which flourished in areas like South America where it did not have the sovereignty of empire to protect it.

The same can be said of the flow of emigrants. There were important British state-sponsored schemes to encourage emigration and schemes for settlement in appropriate colonies. But the impetus which led to the great folk wandering of the nineteenth century did not come from governments. It came from the peoples of Europe, and the flow spread into lands which were not under the flag of the home country of the men and women who were on the move. If it had not been so the development of the United States would have been impossible. As did trade so also emigration needed, on occasion, the protection of European arms. New Zealand and Australia were settled under the protective shield of the British fleet, and in New Zealand and South Africa settlers needed the service of British soldiers to protect them against the natives of the country they were entering, as those who went West in the United States needed the protection of the army of the United States against the Red Indians.

Therefore, though the expansion of European empires, and in particular of the British Empire, forms part of the general process of the expansion of European power and culture and influence in the nineteenth century, it is only part of a much larger movement much of which had little or nothing to do with imperial ambitions, and which very often did not lead to the extension of the area under imperial control.

This fact might indeed be unfortunate. The servants of an empire were normally controlled by rules and in ways in which other agents of expansion, the trader, the prospector or the settler, were not controlled. They had to answer to a public opinion at home which felt a much greater moral responsibility towards indigenous peoples than was likely to be felt by men from Europe, or the United States, pursuing their private interests on the spot. Indeed it seems probable that it was unfortunate when Britain shrank from adding to her imperial responsibilities in an area like the South Pacific where the other agents of expansion were working their will. In fact the extension of imperial rule might supply the only protection and the best government which was at that moment available for peoples who for no fault of their own, were being hustled unceremoniously from the Middle Ages, or the Stone Age, to modern times.

The nature of this colonial or imperial government is of great historic importance. It was one of the most critical points in the relations between Europeans and non-Europeans. Its nature in various countries and at various dates has decided much that has happened in the modern world and affected the nature of many modern governments. It is very desirable that its nature and methods should be studied objectively by scholars who can understand the problems of the governors and the feelings of the governed, and the historic situation in which both were irreducibly involved. Colonial rule was often devoted and responsible and provided not only a better protection for the poor and more just and more rational authority than what preceded it, but it was also more merciful to minority groups or people in opposition than the nationalist régimes that have taken its place. On the other hand it was essentially foreign, sometimes imbued with racial conceit, and as far as the peoples subjected to it were concerned, unrepresentative. Its nature demands very careful reconsideration, but such reconsideration is impossible if everything connected with it is wrapped in one contemptuous term which covers every form of European expansion.

I come back, therefore, to the problem which I suggested at the beginning, the problem of the meaning of the word 'imperialism'. But now it seems necessary to ask a different question about it from that which I asked before. In the first section I asked what had been the meaning of the word in the past and how it had come to acquire the meaning which is now normally attributed to it. I now want to ask what satisfactory use we can make of it. What facts in history can it describe accurately? What uses should be avoided so as to avoid the use of the same word for things which are not identical, or the suggestion of a difference between things which are essentially the same?

As the study of the expansion of Europe has intensified, historians seem to have solved this problem by extending the words 'empire' and 'imperialism' to such an extent that they cover most of the phenomena of expansion. The words have been used to cover any form of extension of influence, or economic expansion, or aggression. As a result of this tendency there has been talk of 'commercial imperialism', the 'imperialism of free trade', 'informal empires' and 'empires of influence and culture'. In fact this usage can be so all-embracing that it is very difficult to see where it should stop, and there is some danger that, since there are no clear logical limitations to the use of the word, the terms of its use will be largely prescribed by interest or bias. There is also a danger that essential differences between policies and actions which can possibly be covered by the words 'empire building' or 'imperialism', if those words are so extended, will be obscured.

For instance, the clashes known as the Opium Wars in China are likely to be cited as examples of 'imperialism', and it may also be said that British trade created an 'informal empire' in South America. Now it will be admitted that the causes of the Opium Wars are not always fully understood, that even the first had less to do with the trade in opium than is usually thought. They were in fact largely caused by the incomprehensions and inconveniences which inevitably developed between an aggressive commercial civilization which had taken the rest of the world for its province, and an ancient political and cultural system which for centuries had been accustomed to regard the outer world as barbarous and to believe that the barbarians who came from without should be treated as tributaries. Anyone trading in China, whether private trader or commercial empire, would have had to face these tensions, and viewed in the categories of world history British expansion in China and British trade in South America are part of the same movement resulting from the same explosive dynamism. But there is one profound difference between the two, the use of force. The door for European trade into China had to be forced open; on the whole this was not true of the door into South America. Emotionally and morally the difference this makes is very great. It meant indeed that some of the most ardent partisans for the expansions of free trade, men like Cobden and Bright, consistently opposed the policies that led to war in China and it seems unfortunate to accept a usage which might include the policies of Cobden, Bright, Palmerston, Elgin, Bowring and Sir Walter Elliot under the same term.

If, however, 'imperialism' is to cover only such expansion as involves force, not only will the word exclude a certain amount of empire building which was relatively peaceful, but it raises the question of circumstances in which the force is exerted not by the policy of a large political unit but by individuals, or made necessary by the actions of individuals, whom the imperial power had tried vainly to restrain. The settler pressing out into native territory, the blackbirder recruiting native labour in the South Seas, these men were not only the agents of European expansion, but they were likely to use, or invoke, force to protect their activities. Yet the only possible restraint on their activities might be the policy of a colonial official, or the reluctant annexation of territory which they infested; again it would seem to confuse matters to use the same emotive abstract term to describe both them and the people who tried to control them.

It may be that a better answer to the problem is to keep the words 'empire', 'imperialist', and 'imperialism' so to speak in inverted commas, to regard them as historic words used by people in a particular period to describe certain institutions, attitudes and activities which should only be applied in ways that people of that period would recognize. This is better historical practice than extending a word far beyond its contemporary meaning, but in this case it presents this difficulty. At any given period these particular words were applied to people and things which are on close inspection essentially different from one another.

Even in Britain in the forty years between 1880 and 1920 the people who could be described as 'imperialists' and the attitudes that could be called 'imperialism' are diverse and sometimes in sharp contrast with each other. There were those who were inspired by a sense of the achievements of the past and their promise for the future. Sometimes this might come from a sober sense of what had been done, or sometimes it might be the romantic echoes of a boyhood's enthusiasm inspired by a popular historian like Fitchett or a novelist like Henty. Sometimes this sense of achievement might inspire a reasonable view of serious responsibilities which could not be evaded, or it could loose those 'wild tongues' of men 'drunk with sight of power', which alarmed Kipling so much at the time of the second jubilee, and inspired a singularly silly desire to paint still more of the map red. Nor were these childish exuberances the only hopes the thought of empire excited. For instance, more dangerous because more rational were the imperialist dreams of a man like Rhodes, 'a united South Africa under Britain', an 'all-British route from the Cape to Cairo', and lurking in the background there might easily be those racial theories which slip into so much of the thought of the later nineteenth or the early twentieth centuries and which, indeed, seem to be in some way embodied in the conception of the Rhodes scholarships.

But there were others who dreamed quite other dreams about the Empire's future. There were for instance those who saw in it the possibility of an association of free peoples, an ideal which started with the idea of a federation of the lands mainly peopled by British stock, but which developed fairly easily into the modern conception of a multi-racial commonwealth. And this idea might itself embody a number of different ideals. There were those who saw this development as desirable in itself and as naturally the next stage in the political evolution of democracy. There were those who saw Armageddon ahead and felt the pull of 'ties of common funk', and there were those who were inspired by the idea of forging the Empire as an economic whole.

This last was, of course, in its way an economic ideal. But it is important to differentiate between those who advocated schemes for the economic development and integration of the Empire which they conceived would benefit everyone, and the capitalists and speculators who were looking for profit in a particular part of the world which they would exploit to their own private advantage. These also had their use for the Empire, and could no doubt from time to time affect its policy. But human motives are mixed and not easily predictable. Even in places and periods in which the desire for private profit was obviously active it would be wrong to assume that it was always the dominant motive. Some of the people with whom Rhodes worked both in Kimberley and in the settlement of Rhodesia were pretty

ruthless operators in whom the desire to make money at whatever cost was strong. Rhodes made use of them, and allowed
them their heads, but he himself was normally inspired by a
wider and less self-centred vision. Whether it was a desirable
vision and whether all that he did in its service is to be commended may very well be debated, but it was not simply a desire
to get rich and it should not be described as if it were.

Again in contrast with Rhodes, and still more with the men
behind him, were those who represented the imperial element
which Rhodes so much disliked. The most eminent of these were
the great colonial proconsuls, men like Sir Hubert Murray in
Papua or Lord Lugard in Nigeria, whose lives were devoted to
safeguarding the perilous passage of the peoples for whom they
were responsible from relatively primitive conditions into the
modern world. Their view of what their task demanded by no
means always corresponded with the wishes of the white settler,
or the great entrepreneur interested in the Empire, as was
demonstrated when Lugard fought the great palm-oil battle with
Lord Leverhulme. Lord Leverhulme wished to introduce large
European-run plantations into Nigeria in order to produce the
oils necessary for making soap. Lugard had come to the conclusion that it was important to keep the European element out of
Nigeria, because it was socially important that the land should
be owned and developed by African farmers, even if that meant
that the economic progress of the territory was slower than it
might otherwise have been. He therefore resisted Lord Leverhulme, and, in spite of all the power Lord Leverhulme could
enlist he lost and had to transfer his plantations to the Congo,
which was outside the British Empire. But the nature of the
'imperial element' should not only be judged by those at the top.
Even more important was the host of hard-working colonial civil
servants, who were prepared to give lifelong responsible service
sometimes in very hard conditions for moderate financial rewards:
whatever the interests of these men they were not those of
planters or company promoters.

Yet all these people might reasonably have been called 'imperialists' and their different aims and ideals might have been
stigmatized as 'imperialism'. In whatever way the word is used
it seems to lead to the confounding of essentially different things

and sharply contrasted people. To this must be added the inconvenience of the strong emotional charge which it carries which often seems to prevent men from considering clearly and rationally any statement into which it is introduced, and the results of the peculiar twist which first Hobson's and then Lenin's use of it gave its meaning. Indeed, there seems to be only one thing to be done and that is to discharge the word 'imperialism' and the words associated with it altogether from one's service, and to describe what has to be described and to discuss what has to be discussed as frankly and accurately as possible without using them at all.

To do so would not imply the acceptance or rejection of any view of the past, or of any particular policy for the world in the future. It would merely be the best way of considering certain important matters without incurring the danger of being deceived by unreal associations and unexamined presuppositions. The words themselves would be no great loss. They are unsatisfactory servants. They are masked words appealing covertly to possibly irrelevant emotions and carrying more meanings than one. They give a common label to things which are different. They deny similarity to things which are certainly the same, and their history is such that any accurate, or honest, use of them is not now practicable.

So dismiss them. There is no need to fear for their future, they will certainly gain employment elsewhere. There are many people who do not particularly want to think clearly in certain contexts.

Cambridge History of the British Empire. Vol. ii, 'The Growth of the New Empire, 1783-1870'. Vol. iii, 'The Empire Commonwealth, 1870-1919'.

Fieldhouse, D. K., 'Imperialism: An Historiographical Revision', *Economic History Review*, vol. xiv, no. 2, 1961.

Gallagher, J., and Robinson, R., with A. Denny, *Africa and the Victorians: The Official Mind of Imperialism.* London, 1961.

Hancock, W. K., *Survey of British Commonwealth Affairs.* Oxford, vol. i, 1937, vol. ii, 1940.

Hobson, J. A., *Imperialism.* London, 1938 (first publ. 1902).

Koebner, R., and Schmidt, H. D., *Imperialism: The Story and Significance of a Political Word, 1840-1960*. Cambridge, 1964.

Lenin, V. I., *Imperialism the Highest Stage of Capitalism* (1916). New ed., London, 1948.

MacDonagh, Oliver, 'The Anti-Imperialism of Free Trade', *Economic History Review*, second series, vol. xiv, no. 3, 1962.

Thornton, A. P., *The Imperial Idea and its Enemies: A Study in British Power*. London, 1959.

See errata page
↓

6

RELIGIOUS AND INTELLECTUAL
DEVELOPMENTS

I NOW WISH TO TURN to some of the effects of the expansive forces of the nineteenth century upon intellectual matters, and as usual it is necessary to start with the population explosion and the industrial revolution. For the population explosion, which doubled and re-doubled the numbers of people in the country may have greatly increased the numbers of potential readers, though it was possibly more likely to have made a greater increase in the number of illiterates, while the improvements in paper making and in the printing press certainly very greatly increase the amount available for them to read.

In the making of paper the crucial invention was that which enabled machine-made paper to supersede hand-made paper, and the change from paper made from rags to paper made from vegetable fibre. The paper making machine was invented in France in 1798, but brought to Britain in 1803. This meant that whereas the old hand mills could produce 50 or 60 lb of paper a day the new mills could produce up to 1,000 lb a day. It also meant that by 1824 the price of some kinds of paper had fallen by a quarter or even a third, and by 1843 by a half. There had been various improvements in the printing-press in the seventeenth and eighteenth centuries, but the real turning point came when the inventions of a German called Friedrich Koenig enabled power to be applied to printing. Perhaps the decisive date is 1814 when *The Times* installed a machine invented by König which enabled 1,100 impressions to be pulled off in an hour as against 300 impressions which was the best the most highly developed hand worked press could do. This was, however, only the beginning of the advance. In 1828 the four-cylinder press invented by Applegath and Cowper gave 4,000 sheets, while in 1848 the rotary press which *The Times* installed gave 8,000, and so on upwards till the rates of 30,000 and 40,000 sheets an hour were achieved in the twentieth century.

König

This enabled the presses to pour out reading matter, much of it very cheap reading matter, in great variety and in an ever increasing flood during the whole of the nineteenth century. Obviously this development was to have important political and social results, but, more than that, it is in itself valuable evidence of contemporary social conditions and social change. One invention aimed at the improved production of a particular article does not follow another in this way unless there is a fair assurance of profit, which probably means an increasing demand for the article to be produced. These inventions therefore imply that there was a rapidly increasing demand for reading matter. As a matter of fact the activities of the booksellers and the development of circulating libraries suggest that that increase had started some way back in the eighteenth century, while the large sales of the works of Walter Scott and Byron show how far things had gone before the end of the first quarter of the century was reached. After that the expansion is at break-neck speed, so fast indeed that it seems clear that, not only had there been changes which enabled literate persons to buy more to read and made them desire to do so, but also that there must have been a great increase in the number of literate persons. This seems to mean that the increase in population did not only increase the illiterate masses in the country, but also increased considerably, for the figures are considerable, the numbers of those who could read and wished to do so.

This, however, raises an interesting and important question. What proportion of the population at any point in the century after the increase of population had got well under way could in fact read and write? On this matter my friend Professor R. K. Webb of Columbia University has thrown a good deal of light. It is a difficult subject, and it would be as well to hesitate before accepting some of the assertions which are confidently made about it by scholars who have not worked at it as systematically as has Professor Webb. Some statements which have ascribed general illiteracy to large sections of the working classes have been no more than perfunctory guesses based on a considerable underestimate of the opportunities for education available for poor people before 1870. Other estimates have been more reasonably based on the number of those who did not sign the register when they married but made their mark. That, however, is to confuse reading with writing. A man who could spell his way through a newspaper might well not be able to write, or to write so fairly that he would like have his name recorded in his own handwriting on such an occasion, particularly if his bride could not read or write at all. In certain sections of society it was probable that she would not be able to do so, since a working class woman was less likely to receive an education than a man. I am afraid that there were a good many people in nine-teenth-century England who thought that women did not need much education, and that it was not good for them.

There were from time to time various systematic attempts to test literacy within particular groups and districts, but they seem normally to set the standard of literacy unrealistically high. A test often applied was whether an individual could read and ex-plain a passage from the Bible. Now the Bible is not an easy book and a good many people who could understand ordinary newspapers might fail on this. Probably there is a general tendency to underestimate the numbers of working class readers at any given date. But any generalization is likely to be mislead-ing. It seems that the proportion of the working class who could read differed markedly in different parts of the country at the same date, and of course still more sharply in different, or even in the same, parts of the country at different dates. Probably as the century went forward and the opportunities for education in-creased in most areas the standard of literacy improved. On the other hand there seems to be some probability that as people wandered about the country in search of work they sometimes lost such chances of learning to read as they might have had in their homes, and that therefore the development of factories and, in particular, of mines, which might bring immigrants into a country district, might mean a decrease in the proportion of literates to illiterates. The matter is complicated by the fact there is in reality no clear line between the fully literate and the illi-terate. There are gradations from the people who cannot read at all through to the people who only read with difficulty, and those who can read but cannot write, or who only write with difficulty, through to the people who have learnt to read perfectly well but who in fact read so seldom that they have practically forgotten

how to do it. It is therefore not really possible to make satisfactory generalizations about the whole century and the whole
country. There are, however, one or two points which can be
made very tentatively.

In the nineteenth century, particularly in the country districts,
there was still a section of society in which an ancient oral
tradition flourished. Many folk-songs, carols, the mummers' play,
the traditional dances survived in England to be collected by
Cecil Sharp and others whom he inspired in the twentieth
century. I myself have seen the mummers' play performed in a
village near Leeds between 1903 and 1914. No doubt when
these things were collected they often came from old men and
old women, but their general spread over the country seems to
suggest that earlier in the nineteenth century there was a large
number of people who enjoyed these things without fear of being
laughed at. The spread of cheap literature and mass produced
songs is the deadly enemy of this kind of culture, and the survival of so much through the century seems to suggest the continued existence of a society in England which lived to itself
and, however many of its members could read, was in some
way cut off from the intellectual currents and fashions of contemporary life.

It would be interesting to learn more about this possibility.
That there was some break in communication is suggested by
the surprise evoked by Cecil Sharp's discoveries themselves. Here
was a rich cultural tradition surviving in the familiar English
countryside of which contemporaries knew little or nothing. It
would be interesting to know whether this ought to be linked
with other points that suggest that town and countryside, or that
certain elements in the town and certain elements in the country,
although they may seem to be of the same class and in other
ways like minded, found it difficult to communicate with one
another. For instance, some of the studies of Chartism seem to
suggest that in some counties Chartist activities did not spread
with ease into the deep countryside. Where there is Chartist
activity in the country it seems to affect men employed at a
small factory, or in a coal-mine, or in some other suburban
pocket, and not agricultural labourers in their traditional sur-
roundings. Yet often enough agricultural labourers had, if any-

thing, more serious grievances than the men in the towns and resented them more fiercely, as seems to be shown by the incidence of rural incendiarism. If there is anything in all this it would be interesting to know how the popular religious bodies who flourished in the countryside, Baptists, Primitive Methodists, Congregationalists, were related to this ancient culture.

This group probably should not be confused with a different and more desolate group more likely to be found in the towns. There were the people who could not read and had lost whatever they might have had to take the place of reading. There were for instance the poor factory children whose absolute ignorance even of the names of the chief figures in the Gospels so shocked people in the first half of the nineteenth century. There were many of the people whom Mayhew interviewed. There were the people whose ignorance Dickens recognized and feared, or those who feature in many reports on home missions. This was the real world of the uprooted. In that dark world literacy or any awareness of the ideas which literacy brings must have been rare indeed.

These two groups were clearly outside the sphere of the ordinary current of literate ideas, and there seem to have been others who were indeed able to read but were hardly in it. Charles Knight was a man who was deeply interested in the whole question of working class reading, and he superintended the publications of the Society for the Diffusion of Useful Knowledge and edited the *Penny Cyclopaedia*. He reported that much of the working class spent their time reading a type of literature which he found it hard to displace in favour of what he felt was worth-while. This seems to be intelligible, indeed some of this literature has survived. It was a literature of sensational novels, rather violent newsprints with a great many descriptions of murders and prize-fights and executions, and ballads which describe the same kind of thing, including at least in the first half of the century that old favourite item, the last dying confessions of executed murderers. A certain amount of pornography, sometimes in ballad form, has survived which might be part of this literature, but I suppose it would be impossible to say for whom it was intended.

If these people are left aside, however, there remains the large public which was taking up greedily the increasing mass of more civilized reading matter which the new processes were providing. This body must have included all those who were articulate or responsive to the movements of opinion and thought in the nation. What proportion of the nation it comprised it would be difficult to say, particularly since its boundaries were not quite the same as those who could read and those who could not do so. Probably a considerable number of the unskilled labourers and also many agricultural labourers, however rich their own culture, should be excluded from this public. Otherwise it is probably wrong to define it in terms of economic or social class. There was certainly a fully literate section of the working class, particularly in Scotland. The Chartist paper the *Northern Star*, published in Leeds in the 1830s and 1840s, was clearly written for an intelligent public well aware of what was going on in the intellectual life of the country. On the other hand there were no doubt men and women, particularly women, who were in a better economic position than any member of the working class but did not read much, or only read what was very crude. In any case it is surely a mistake to believe that people in apparently the same economic position, or even with the same educational advantages, necessarily read the same things or reach the same cultural level. Probably, therefore, the best way to analyse the reading public is not by trying to guess from what class they sprang where that is not reasonably clear, but by considering what they were like from the literature provided for them.

For instance, the substantial nineteenth-century reviews, the *Edinburgh*, the *Quarterly* and the rest, in which so many important controversies were conducted, must have catered for an educated public prepared to consider long articles embodying reasonably difficult arguments and carrying quite abstruse literary allusions; indeed the number and prosperity of these magazines suggest that the serious reading public was proportionately larger, when compared with the whole mass of readers, than it is today. In the middle of the century *The Times* was the most important newspaper. It was expensive and as compared with the numbers of population, or even with the numbers which were sold of a publication like the *Penny Cyclopaedia*, its circulation figures do not look large and the importance of the influence it exerted perhaps suggests how large a part in the affairs of the nation was played by a very small number of people. This conclusion may, however, be rather deceptive, for there was in most towns and counties a flourishing provincial press which not only gave voice to a vigorous local opinion and much space to local news but always copied from the London papers, including *The Times* with a lavishness which might not now seem to be proper. Perhaps it can be assumed that the readers of *The Times* and the more substantial magazines were in the upper and best educated classes.

In the middle of the century the most popular novelist was probably Dickens, and the variety of his admirers seems to suggest that some identity of taste and feeling prevailed through a larger section of the reading public than it did in the last quarter of the century when more exacting critical standards had developed and literary snobbery was on the increase. For instance, men who might have been expected to have been rather drastic critics admired passages in Dickens like the death of little Nell, or of Paul Dombey, which their counterparts fifty years later would have rejected with contumely. This uniformity of taste no doubt gave a reasonable public to other novelists of genius and talent in the middle of the century, and possibly explains elements in the art of such writers as Thackeray and George Eliot which would not have existed if they had been writing for a smaller more sophisticated body of readers. But of course it is in the cruder popular novelists that an image of the mass of the nineteenth-century reading public can be seen most clearly. They reflect its prudery, its snobbery, as in the novels of the 'silver fork' school, its love of melodrama, its religiosity and its emotionalism. That emotionalism, and that religiosity, also overflowed into the very large amount of poetry which got itself published. For not only was printing cheap for an aspirant poet and the pages of magazines and newspapers hospitable, but there was obviously a large public prepared to enjoy the work of a fluent and lachrymose poet like Mrs Hemans, or a passionate one like Letitia Landon.

Much of the reading matter was specifically religious; indeed, each religious party or denomination tended to enjoy literature written to suit it. There were Evangelical novels, the best known of which is I suppose the *Fairchild Family*, and High Church novels, like the works of Charlotte M. Yonge. There were innumerable denominational newspapers and magazines. On the Church side, possibly the most scholarly was the *British Critic*, and on the Dissenting side, the *Eclectic Review*. Others were more fanatical, as was the Evangelical paper the *Record*, which took pleasure in lambasting such clergymen as showed a deplorable tendency not to believe in Hell. According to Matthew Arnold the oracle of wisdom for many Nonconformists was the *British Banner*, whose intellectual claims he, characteristically, put lower than those of the *Saturday Review*, which was originally a High Church newspaper but was open to a mixed group of lawyers and intellectuals who took a peculiar delight in lambasting Nonconformists.

In fact, though the mass of what was published in Britain in the nineteenth century demonstrates many of the common characteristics of the public, it also shows very clearly the innumerable divisions and sub-divisions, normally, at least nominally, religious, which cut it up. And there were some walls of partition cutting off some sections of it which seem at first sight to be impermeable. This fact is exemplified by the history of two poets called Montgomery, James Montgomery and Robert Montgomery, who was also called 'Devil' Montgomery because he wrote a poem on the Devil. James Montgomery was the editor of the Sheffield *Iris*, and had been the victim of Tory persecution at the outset of his career. He was a dullish poet. I would not advise any prolonged reading of 'The Wanderer in Switzerland' or 'The World before the Flood', which were considered to be his masterpieces. His best poems are hymns, some of which are sung today such as 'Angels from the Realms of Glory', or 'Hail to the Lord's Anointed'. He had, however, a very considerable reputation largely among the Methodists and the Moravians, and the *Eclectic Review* believed him to be one of the greatest poets of the day. 'Devil' Montgomery, who also wrote on 'The Omnipresence of the Deity', was the worse poet of the two. Where James is dull, Robert is absurd. Where James falls back into mediocre piety, Robert plunges headlong into furious nonsense. Their popularity seemed to be a scandal and two leading critics of the day determined to destroy them. Jeffrey, the editor of the *Edinburgh Review* gave James Montgomery a thorough drubbing in his magazine with the idea of extinguishing him and Macaulay produced, also in the *Edinburgh Review,* an article on Robert Montgomery which has since become famous. Robert Montgomery's florid excesses and confused metaphors laid him open to the exposure of verbal inconsistencies which Macaulay conceived to be a large part of literary criticism, and to the kind of bludgeon work in which he excelled. He took full advantage of his opportunities with intent to kill. Both poets were extremely angry at the treatment they had received, indeed Robert, who had already been severely handled in *Fraser's Magazine*, seems to have thought of sueing Macaulay. But the interesting point is that however ruffled at the time neither poet was in the end a penny the worse. The work of James which Jeffrey had attacked went on to a ninth edition and he made £800 out of it. Robert's nonsense on 'The Omnipresence of the Deity', which was only in the eleventh edition when Macaulay wrote, went on to its twenty-eighth edition. There was obviously a large public which cared nothing for neither Jeffrey or Macaulay, if they had even heard of them.

Considering the eminence and influence of each of those critics this is remarkable and points to a dividing line in the mind of the country which may explain one of the oddest facts in its intellectual and spiritual history. What may reasonably be called the crisis of the nineteenth-century attack on religion came between 1859 and 1871. In 1859 Darwin's *Origin of Species* appeared. In 1860 seven English churchmen published *Essays and Reviews* in which certain orthodox doctrines were questioned. In 1862 Bishop Colenso started to publish his doubts about the Pentateuch. In 1863 Sir Charles Lyell produced his evidence on the antiquity of man, which seemed to be inconsistent with the account of creation in the Bible. In 1863 Renan's humanizing *Vie de Jésus* appeared. In 1865 J. R. Seeley of Cambridge published another humanizing work on Christ called *Ecce Homo.* In 1870 the British Association at Exeter generally accepted evolution. In 1871 Darwin produced his *Descent of*

Man. Thus in these ten to twelve years orthodox religion received a series of body blows, which seemed to be aimed at its existence.

The reactions were violent. In 1860 Bishop Wilberforce made his unfortunate attempt to kill Darwinism by ridicule at the meeting of the British Association. The authors of *Essays and Reviews,* one of whom was a future Archbishop of Canterbury, were called the *Septem contra Christum,* the seven against Christ, and an attempt was made to secure their official condemnation. The outcry against Colenso was tremendous, and his Archbishop excommunicated him and made an unsuccessful attempt to depose him. In 1866 when the good Lord Shaftesbury was speaking at the Church Pastoral Aid Society he denounced *Ecce Homo* as 'the most pestilential book ever vomited from the jaws of Hell'. He admitted afterwards that what he had said was perhaps a little strong, or rather as he said 'too strong for the world, but not too strong for truth, justifiable and yet injudicious'. It is not easy for us to comprehend this state of mind, it is not easy for us to understand why these works caused such intense anger and fear: but then we have not been brought up in a world where Biblical literalism is taken for granted and considered to be the foundation of faith. Given the circumstances of that time I think we must take it that it was reasonable for sensible men to believe that revealed religion was in the greatest danger.

Yet this is precisely the period of the great religious revivals. They start in northern Ireland in 1859 and they go by devious routes over England, Scotland and Wales. The years between 1860 and 1870 are known among the Baptists as the Revival Decade, when more Baptist churches were founded in London than in any other ten years. All through this period Spurgeon, who was a very old-fashioned theologian, was drawing enormous crowds to his tabernacle in London. In 1873 Sankey and Moody invaded Britain from the United States. In 1875 the Salvation Army began to take on its final shape.

Clearly then in the Britain of the nineteenth century literate groups could exist without much effective communication with each other. This probably ought to make it difficult to consider the spiritual and intellectual history of Britain in this crowded and complicated period of ebullient growth as a whole. The usual answer to this problem seems to be to select a succession of eminent people to study in order to plot a path through the century, and perhaps it is not unfair to say that they do very often seem to be the same people—Bentham, Coleridge, Carlyle, Newman, John Stuart Mill, possibly Darwin, possibly Huxley, possibly Walter Bagehot, certainly Matthew Arnold, probably George Eliot. Except for Newman, it is not usual to include Christian theologians and scholars, and still less the great Christian preachers. It is generally held that these people are below the salt intellectually and therefore can be neglected. I find this difficult to accept. Among these people were men of considerable intelligence and also men of great power. The men and women who were drawn to such leaders probably excelled in numbers those who attended to many of the great writers who are normally considered, and I cannot think that in this matter anything human should be alien to our studies. But even putting aside as irrelevant and not worth consideration the feelings and beliefs of more than half of humanity, there still seems to be a tendency in the normal treatment to be eclectic, to concentrate too exclusively on certain favourite personalities and themes, and to neglect others which may well have an equal claim to consideration.

It may be easiest to make this point clear by considering the way the history of British Universities has been treated. To take Oxford as an example, much has been written on Newman and his Oxford, and work has been done on Jowett and Mark Pattison. But leaving them on one side there is very little on the intellectual history of the Oxford of the half century after Newman went away, an Oxford which produced in T. H. Green and F. H. Bradley, two of the most interesting of nineteenth-century British philosophers, and had in Stubbs one of its best professional historians, an Oxford whose influence on British politics and still more on British administration was all important. Or to turn to Cambridge, there are, it is true, D. A. Winstanley's important series of volumes, but they are concerned with organization and personalities, not with intellectual history. A certain amount has been written about Tennyson and the Apostles, or about some of the Apostles. Leslie Stephen has been carefully studied, and there has already been a certain amount, and there is clearly going to be more, on Lord Keynes and the Bloomsbury Phalanx. But there is as yet nothing modern on the intellectual activities of Whewell, who was a remarkable and influential man, or on Adam Sedgwick. There is nothing sufficient on Connop Thirlwall, or on Lightfoot, or on Westcott. There is very little on Henry Sidgwick who was, among other things, with Gurney, Myers and Verrall, one of the pioneers of psychical research. Maitland's position in the history of scholarship has not perhaps been fully considered. Nor is there anything adequate on the recovery of the natural sciences and mathematics at Cambridge, which placed that University again in the front rank of European thought, an event one might have thought of an importance comparable with the Oxford Movement about which so much has been written. Or, to turn from Oxford and Cambridge, not enough has been written about Edinburgh and Glasgow, whose importance in the intellectual life of Britain in the early nineteenth century can hardly be exaggerated, not yet about University College, London, which trained such people as R. H. Hutton and Walter Bagehot.

I only speak of the Universities, not because they played an overwhelmingly important part in the history of British nineteenth-century culture, but because they offer a convenient way of showing how easy it is for much that is possibly of considerable significance to be left out of the picture. What is selected for study is at least in part selected by accident. What often happens is probably that one writer naturally follows where others have gone before, and the rabble rout of thesis writers and men and women seeking Ph.D. degrees, either follow their masters or choose subjects for the intelligible but insufficient reason that they are not likely to have been chosen by anyone else. All this may be a natural method of selection, but it does not necessarily lead to the survival of the fittest. It is, however, difficult to see what other method will certainly lead to the selection of what is most significant and important in the thought of so rich and various a century.

For one thing it seems clear that it would be wrong to concentrate only on the thought which now seems to be interesting and important to us. There were people in the nineteenth century the interest of whose ideas has completely faded, who never-theless in their day exercised very great influence. Herbert Spencer is not without interest as an individual. His innocent, but quite unbounded, vanity, his naïve attempt to make that hard woman, Beatrice Potter as she then was, Beatrice Webb as she became, devote herself to writing his life and editing his works, such curious habits as the ear flaps which he let down at a given point in the evening lest he should hear more and be unable to sleep—all these things make up a character of consider-able comedy interest. However, it is, I suppose, forty or so years since anyone except readers on the periphery of civilization has taken his work seriously, or willingly read it. Yet in his day he had an influence as great, or greater, than Karl Marx, and any discussion of English thought which excludes him is obviously incomplete.

Nor yet can one afford to fail to pay attention to what in the terms of modern orthodoxy seems absurd and outrageous. In fact, I think one of the most interesting facts about the nine-teenth century is the large number of people, often intelligent and reasonably well educated people, who followed paths which apparently led into the inane. Nowadays Professors of Phren-ology, the science of ascertaining the mental and the moral qualities of a man from the bumps on his head, are relegated to the booths of fair grounds, where they share rather humble accommodation with ladies who do the same form of divination from the palm of the hand. But in the early part of the nine-teenth century, Richard Cobden believed in phrenology and in various mechanics' institutes there were opportunities for intelli-gent mechanics to study it. Homoeopathic medicine was widely believed in and practised in the middle of the century. It prob-ably saved lives, but it saved them because it saved patients from the hands of the orthodox practitioner with his heroic purgings and bleedings and only inflicted on them remedies which did nothing at all. The doctrines it embodied were not those which science was to confirm. Yet in the nineteenth century it was accepted by educated people whose critical intelligence is by no means to be despised.

More interesting still because it has a double significance, is the history of research into the phenomena of hypnosis. These phenomena had been observed and used by Mesmer in the eighteenth century, but he was hounded out of orthodox medicine first in Vienna and then in Paris, and the subject was driven out into the wilderness. During the nineteenth century the phenomena of hypnosis and suggestion were explored and hypnotism practised by a good many people; but, as was inevitable in the circumstances, they were most of them men and women whose beliefs were on the edge, or beyond, the frontiers of the world of ordinary educated thought. Many of them were in fact jugglers and quacks who had lighted on something which they could exploit, while others were genuine faith healers, who had discovered that they had certain powers which they could use to effect cures and relieve suffering. There were, however, also perfectly normal medical men who were prepared to experiment in something which might be important. But they risked their professional career if they did so, for the medical profession in general so disliked the subject that it seems to have been prepared to ruin anyone who was known to dabble in it.

Further beyond the frontiers of orthodox science there were the spiritualists and beyond them the theosophists, the occultists, the fabricators of new religions, and a whole host of other visionaries of some sort or another. There were also people who produced new theories about economics and politics and history. A good many variations on themes provided by Christianity appeared from time to time as also variations on themes provided by science or rationalism, particularly after Darwinism had provided a jargon both attractive and adaptable. There was of course a great deal of fraud and folly at work here, but it is remarkable how many intelligent and at least reasonably educated men adopted positions which seemed then, or may seem now, to be intellectually beyond the pale. For instance, a number of highly intelligent people believed in spiritualism, while those who took the results of psychical research seriously included some of the most remarkable men and women of the last quarter of the nineteenth century.

Those engaged in psychical research, however, should perhaps be separated from the wild company of the other heretics; for they were not enthusiastic amateurs engaged in speculations which they had not sufficient critical discipline to control, but

highly educated men and women pursuing a carefully considered
line of investigation, investigations which have indeed produced
results which orthodox opinion has had to take much more
seriously than orthodox opinion in the nineteenth century was
prepared to do. This is obviously also true of those who experi-
mented in hypnosis, or, to go to a completely different field, of
some writers on economic subjects who were damned as un-
orthodox.

Be that as it may, if the picture is taken as a whole it is one
of immense vitality and very great variety. It was inherently
likely that it should be like that. There was an ever increasing
mass of reading matter, there was an ever increasing body of
readers. Many of these were highly intelligent men and women,
but they often had had an inadequate education, or practically
no education, and they seem often to have worked out their own
ideas beyond the effective range of exterior criticism. However,
even for those who were in close touch with educated thought
the number of acceptable varieties of thought seems to have been
greater than it is today. For one thing, there did not exist the
vast mass of scientific discovery which stands today, or rather
seems to stand, between a modern man and so many possible
lines of speculation. Moreover, many intelligent and educated
men and women founded their basic beliefs upon the authority
of the Bible in a way that few people now would accept, and so
came to adopt positions to which their counterparts today would
not give a thought, positions which would not now be conceived
to be within the possible compass of sane educated opinion.

The result was a teeming and confused mass of creeds, or
theories, about the universe and mankind. Some of these were
produced by thinkers whom we recognize, some by men of whom
we know nothing, or ignore. It may be possible to select from
all this body of thinkers certain men and women and to say that
these were significant, their thought was the thought of educated
and critical people, and that the rest can be neglected. I do not
myself think that this would be easy, and I am quite certain I
would not want to do this. It seems to me that the whole scene,
as far as we can survey it, is of great interest in the history of
humanity, and also in the history of thought. I would, therefore, rather not try to answer the question what we are to select

from all this mass, but rather two related questions. First, what light do these varieties of opinion and literature throw upon the nature of the social and intellectual groups which made up nineteenth-century society and their relations with each other. And, second, are there any common factors which penetrate the whole mass or a large part of it? I have tried to touch upon some aspects of the first question, and I believe there is much still to be done. The second is a difficult question, but I wish to suggest two ways in which an attempt might be made to answer it.

The first is the obvious one of trying to detect in contemporary achievements and activities some common element which they all share. The second is to judge by results, that is, to consider opinion in the twentieth century and to try to see whether men and women of different traditions and groups did in fact tend to come to the same ways of thinking on certain important points in the end.

For the purpose of the arrangement of my matter I wish to take the second of these methods first. The point at which it is best to start is, I believe, this. If you were to take any large group of literate, tolerably educated, people between 1850 and 1860, or possibly later in the century, you would find that the majority of them believed, or made as if to believe, that the world had been created in six days, that our first parents were Adam and Eve, and that there had been a world-wide flood and that Noah had preserved selections of all things living in the Ark. If you took the same body of persons at any moment in the last forty years you would be very unlikely to find any who held those opinions, even if they were all professing Christians. Something had happened. The conclusions of the nineteenth-century scientists from Lyell to Huxley, aided by the work of the anthropologists, the archaeologists and the Biblical scholars seemed in some way to have got home to everyone, in spite of the fact that when that work appeared three quarters of the country repudiated the ideas it inspired and anathematized those who popularized them, or else were apparently unaffected by the whole matter.

Something had happened to make ordinary people adjust their basic beliefs. Sometimes they did this after a struggle, sometimes unconsciously, or while pretending that nothing was happening.

I think the reason for this change was the fact that throughout the last century the wind of criticism was blowing fiercely, and that it penetrated everywhere, passing through apparently impermeable walls of faith or prejudice by routes of which men were often completely unaware.

It was not only the wind raised by intelligent scientists, for the popular criticism of accepted beliefs had gone on ceaselessly from early in the century. Apart from the humble practitioners in places like Hyde Park there were the professional secularists like Holyoake or Bradlaugh or Mrs Besant, and I suspect that Bradlaugh and Mrs Besant were two of the most effective public speakers that the nineteenth century produced.

Nor, as I see it, was the most dangerous criticism of Christianity that of the scientists. That became in due course very formidable and as it developed, was warmly welcomed by the forces which were already engaged in the assault. But the criticisms of science and of Darwinism had been preceded by other arguments against Christianity as it was then understood, which were more deadly and more universal in their appeal. They were the arguments against the morality of the creed received from the Bible. People were repelled on moral grounds by the savagery with which Jehovah had apparently ordered his people to treat those who opposed them. They could not accept as compatible with divine beneficence the injunction in Exodus that 'thou shalt not suffer a witch to live', or the slaying of the prophets of Baal at the brook Kishon, or the two bears who destroyed the forty and two children who mocked at Elisha, or Christ's curse on a fig tree for not bearing fruit out of due season. Above all, more and more people were revolted by the dreadful doctrine of an eternity of torture for the wicked or for the unlucky.

These objections did not have to wait to be endorsed by the doctrine of evolution, and, from early in the century, seem to have provided the pabulum on which most street corner attacks on Christianity were based. The orthodox struggled stubbornly against these criticisms: eminent Anglicans contended fiercely for their right to be eternally damned, enlightened Scots Professors developed carefully argued cases to show that it was peculiarly just and proper for God to order Saul to slaughter all the Amalekites. But it was no good. The whisper in the wind was: 'You are talking nonsense and pretty ugly nonsense at that'. So surreptitiously they began to slip away from what were, in the light of the humanity of that day, untenable positions. A friend of mine who is working on revivalist hymns tells me that during the first three quarters of the nineteenth century the doctrine of Hell, which had been of such use to earlier revivalists was gradually toned down and dropped out until in the 1870s at the time of the activities of Sankey and Moody it had almost entirely disappeared. It seems to be a symbol of very much that was happening, especially in the last quarter of the nineteenth and the first quarter of the twentieth century.

The incessant public discussion of the nineteenth century and the great mass of reading matter therefore gave voice to a body of ideas which were not only numerous and various but on some matters pervasive. In the atmosphere of that day certain arguments were hard to resist and, even if a man refused to pay attention to what was being argued, he was nevertheless likely to be unconsciously affected through what he read or listened to, when there was so much to read or to listen to. Therefore, even though the walls or partitions which divided the public were strong, though in order to resist ideas they disliked men tried to erect on what Mr Gladstone called 'the impregnable rock of Holy Scripture' a fortification with embrasures through which the wrath of God could be conveniently discharged in every direction, in the end there were few corners into which the wind of criticism had not forced an entrance.

The result is the state of opinion today. Most men have lost from their grasp some of the myths which used to be generally believed. Whether this is altogether a good thing, or not, is a matter of opinion. Unfortunately men have not really moved from ways of thought founded on myth to ways of thought founded on rational criticism. It does not seem that many people have mastered the methods of systematic criticism; what most people have done is to accept the result of other people's criticism, and probably a new set of myths into the bargain.

It may indeed be that for a variety of reasons the simile of the *wind* of criticism is not satisfactory. Apart from everything else a wind blows in many directions, but perhaps a better simile would be that of a river which moves only in one. Perhaps the best picture of the setting of nineteenth-century opinion would be that of a broad river with a strong current. The breast of the river is full of boats, some of them go rapidly downstream, some of them sail across the river, some laboriously pull or tack upstream. But the current runs swiftly, so that unless a man is very obstinate, or very lucky, he will infallibly end nearer the sea than when he started.

I believe this gives some similitude of the movement of opinion in the century. Viewed from the vantage point of the 1960s it seems to be moving irresistibly in one direction, carrying with it both all those who desire to go that way and also most of those who do not. It moves from long accepted mythology towards what purport to be rational beliefs based on scientific discovery, from primitive callousness towards a rejection of cruelty both in practice and in the subject matter of religious beliefs, from an acceptance of the values of an hierarchical society based largely on hereditary privilege towards a belief in the absoluteness of human equality, from a trust in traditional forms of government towards the acceptance of the inalienable and irresistible rights of popular majorities. Many men were naturally hesitant about these changes. They resisted the developments in religion, they feared the movement towards democracy. There was much conservative writing in the century, and some conservative thought, a most trenchant and intelligent example of which Sir James Fitzjames Stephen's *Liberty, Equality, Fraternity*. But the movement stopped for no man, and by 1900 few people were likely to advance the propositions or even entertain the prejudices which were commonly advanced, or entertained, before 1830.

Various separate elements can perhaps be discerned in this movement, the development of rationalism, the impact of scientific discovery, an increased sensibility, the rejection of prescription as a source of rights in favour of a system based on the absolute rights of a common humanity. Whether all these elements are themselves facets of one all embracing spirit of the age is a problem I am not capable of considering. Nor can I guess whether the movement will always go forward in the same direction. There is indeed one matter in which the advance of the nineteenth century does not seem to be continued into our own century. The Britain of the mid-nineteenth was much more deeply religious than mid-eighteenth century Britain, but mid-twentieth century Britain is not as religious as was the Britain of the nineteenth century. This suggests that at least one common element in intellectual life of the last century may not be easy to detect by considering the aftermath of the period. If such an element exists, therefore, it must be sought by direct inspection, and I propose to devote my next lecture to the discussion of such a possibility. The element in the intellectual and spiritual life of the country which I shall try to consider I shall call 'romanticism' or 'the romantic element'.

Arnold, Matthew, *Culture and Anarchy*. Cambridge, 1950 (first publ. 1869).

Eiseley, Loren, *Darwin's Century: Evolution and the Man who Discovered it*. New York, 1961.

Faber, Geoffrey, *Jowett: A Portrait with a Background*. London, 1957.

Houghton, W. E., *The Victorian Frame of Mind; 1830-1870*. New Haven, 1957.

Mill, J. S., *On Liberty*. First publ. 1859.

Richter, Melvin, *The Politics of Conscience: T. H. Green and his Age*. London, 1964.

Willey, Basil, *More Nineteenth Century Studies: A Group of Honest Doubters*. London, 1956.

7

ROMANTICISM

THE DIFFICULTY which attaches to the word 'romanticism' is, as any student of literature will tell you, that it can mean so many different things: in fact an American scholar has suggested that we ought to talk, not about romanticism, but about romanticisms in the plural. There are, however, I think, certain characteristics common to most romanticisms which make it possible to talk about romanticism as an entity in history, and I believe that the best way to start doing so is to see romanticism as a reaction against the factors which had been dominant in the intellectual and spiritual history of the period which lasted roughly from some point in the second half of the seventeenth century to the last quarter of the eighteenth. Those factors had been a belief in reason with a strong predilection for common sense, a dislike both of fanaticism and what they called by the technical name of 'enthusiasm', a word which had a profounder and a more precise meaning than it has today, and an admiration for what could be considered classical.

These tendencies helped to produce an intellectual climate which emphasized in religion the importance of morality rather than the claims of the spiritual life, and in the arts of correctness, regularity and form. Intellectual and spiritual progress often, I believe, derives from men stressing the opposite to what their fathers believed. The climate of the eighteenth century had, at least in part, come into existence owing to a reaction against the passions that had ravaged the sixteenth and earlier seventeenth century, the ecstacies and miseries of the Reformation and Counter-Reformation. Romanticism was a reaction against that reaction.

Perhaps the most profound element in romanticism so conceived was the reaction against reason, or what the eighteenth century conceived to be 'reason'. The whole conception of reason presents difficult problems. But men in the earlier eighteenth century tended to believe in the conclusive results of a process

107

of ratiocination based on limited premises fortified by common sense. The objections to the assumptions on which this was based were forcibly stated by David Hume, the philosopher. Moreover as the eighteenth century drew to its end more and more people came to feel, for a variety of causes, that the old habits of mind had seriously limited the human vision, and that matters of great importance to humanity could only be revealed by the heart, or spirit, or imagination, or whatever term you like to use for those faculties of the mind which are not strictly rational.

What men tried to say when they were discussing this was often based on experience rather than on disciplined argument, and the terms they used were often obscure and equivocal, such as a professional philosopher nowadays would find it difficult to pass. But it is more important to try to understand what they felt than to subject what they said to accurate, and no doubt destructive, verbal analysis. For this reason it is best to consider their actual artistic achievement rather than any theory that may have been used to justify or explain it. It was, in fact, natural that romanticism should find its expression more completely in poetry than in prose, and in Britain among the pioneers of romanticism were some of the greatest poets who have written in English: Wordsworth, Coleridge, Shelley, Blake and Keats, with Byron hanging uneasily between the old and the new. Their poetry was in striking contrast to the work of some of the leading poets of the preceding age, such as Pope and Boileau, a contrast so great that men developed the habit of saying that those earlier poets had not been poets at all. For the romantic vision could only be made possible by a revolution, both in treatment and in aim, in the arts, not in poetry alone but in painting and music as well. It was a revolution by which the range of emotion and human experience that could be explored was greatly enlarged, and it is probably by considering what that revolution did, and what it produced, that it is easiest to understand what romanticism was.

There is a case that it revealed truths about man and eternity which the old dispensation could not have revealed. It also, certainly, produced new sources of pleasure, and it did this at a moment when those pleasures were not to be restricted to a small literate minority but would be extended to larger numbers of people than ever before. As I mentioned previously, in the early years of the nineteenth century improvements in the making of paper and in printing, and the enterprise of publishers and booksellers, made much larger circulations of magazines and books possible, with the result that some of the great romantic writers in Britain, such as Lord Byron and Sir Walter Scott, reached a wider public than perhaps any writers had reached before their day. These opportunities were not only available for the great. The presses teemed with the work of much lesser writers, in fact I believe it to be important to consider the romantic movement not only as a movement of the élite which inspired some of the most important writers of all times, but also as a popular movement, which affected a large section of the population, and which incidentally produced some of the worst writers of whom there is record.

For as a popular movement romanticism had its unavoidable weakness. The emotions may reveal truths which systematic ratiocination would never reach, but emotion for the sake of emotion is also a natural source of pleasure, and the things which can be used to stimulate emotion can be either morbid, or absurd, or both. This taste for emotionalism has always been present in human minds, but it seems possible that in the first half of the nineteenth century men and women learnt now to exploit it as it had never been exploited before. They could also do this for the benefit of a larger audience than had ever existed before. The opportunities presented by the new facilities for mass publication as they developed, greatly increased the company of writers, but did not improve their quality. The resources of emotionalism and sensationalism were used to the full. Many poems and songs harped on the idea of death. Many poems and stories portrayed the paroxysms of hopeless love or the wilder passions such as the desire for revenge or the profounder depths of despair. In order that emotions could be displayed which were more powerful than ordinary human beings were likely to generate outsize heroes and heroines were often created. They were credited with sins which were blacker, virtues which were whiter and passions which were less manageable than those of ordinary men and women, and they lived lives which were more calamitous and dramatic than the usual chances of life make probable.

The vicarious enjoyment of unusually powerful emotions and the contemplation of violent and terrifying events no doubt provided for many people a welcome escape from the humdrum of ordinary nineteenth-century existence and this was also provided by the exotic background in time and place which appeared to provide the appropriate scenery for beings and situations which were so far from the usual, that it was really necessary to locate them in some district or period where the ordinary probabilities of life did not prevail and where the common sense rules which control and hamper normal conduct operated only intermittently. Such scenery could be found in the contemporary world. In the early nineteenth century there still survived many untidy districts where these conditions could be presumed, but if these did not suffice there was always the past, particularly the Middle Ages, an attractive period of which not much was known except that during its course men wore armour, talked fustian and were activated by the most extravagant motives and the Church, particularly the religious orders, harboured some very queer people indeed.

Therefore a good many districts, envisaged at suitable periods in their history, served to stimulate this taste for the exotic. There was Calabria with its brigands, Greece in the state of picturesque ruin to which the Turks had reduced it, the Levant with the possibly of pirates. There were the Apennines with heaven knows what going on in the castles which clung to their slopes, and the Alps with their precipices and avalanches where the virtuous and heroic Swiss might serve as a foil to such strangers as the dark beings burdened with mysterious sins who wandered in their midst. And there was the Black Forest, enriched by German folklore and sentiment, with its charcoal burners, its gloomy recesses among the fir trees and its wolves and witches.

Byron, though he also wrote poetry of genius, fully satisfied these cravings, and he had many imitators. There was also in the last years of the eighteenth and the early years of the nineteenth century a brisk trade in horror novels such as supplied titles for the Minerva Press or were satirized in Jane Austen's

Northanger Abbey. They were sufficiently absurd, but the cult of the medieval brought into the field a man who was naturally saner and possessed a much greater sense of reality than most of those who were dabbling in romantic history. Sir Walter Scott did on occasion write the ordinary rubbish. In *The Monastery* he used a peculiarly silly lay figure from the romantic property basket in the White Lady of Avernel. In *Anne of Geierstein* he employed much of the normal paraphernalia of romanticism: the Swiss, the mysterious strangers who sought hospitality among them, who if they were not in this case unpardonable offenders were at least disguised noblemen, a black garbed priest who appeared and disappeared with startling results at unexpected moments, and the society of the Rosy Cross. He could also by mixing together the habits, language and institutions of many different centuries in one glorious confusion produce a vigorous pantomime of historical nonsense like *Ivanhoe*. These things served to show his affinities. When, however, he gave his innate powers a chance, as when he was dealing with a period near enough to his own time for him to understand, the eighteenth and even the seventeenth centuries, above all when he dealt with people whom he knew and loved as he did the people of the Scottish countryside over which he travelled so often as sheriff, then indeed he became a great novelist and wrote with penetration and a feeling for reality and truth which was quite foreign to the work of the ordinary romantic novelists.

Indeed his genius helped to add a new dimension to history. His feeling for what was different from the fashions of his own day was strong enough to make him see that people who lived in other ages and places had had minds which moved in ways that were fundamentally different from the ways of the minds of his contemporaries in Britain, a fact which I believe Edward Gibbon, great historian as he was, never fully realized about the people of whom he wrote. Moreover, Scott's sense of reality prevented him from sacrificing all common humanity to the exotic as did so many romantic writers. This led to the development of what was the great contribution of romanticism to history, the sense of the special characteristics of a period, or the special characteristics of a nation.

Walter Scott's influence was very great. He was widely read

and widely copied not only in Britain, but in France, and Germany, and also for that matter in the United States. It is true that, in Britain at least, they were apt to copy his weakest side for they knew no better; indeed the od's bodikins forsoothery which he introduced into his weaker medieval novels provided a language and a type of behaviour which become common form in any number of historical novels through the rest of the century. That, however, did not reduce his influence, it enhanced it, for it made it more likely that work by him, or copied from him as a model, would be readily conveyed by the new methods of mass production to the new mass audience.

For his importance as a writer does not only depend on his excellence as a novelist, it also derives from the size of his public; the same is even more true of Charles Dickens, and the rapid improvement of the facilities for printing and publishing had important results for other forms of romantic literature. As I said earlier, the cheapness of printing made it easy for aspiring poets to get their works before the public, as the history of the Tennyson brothers or of the Brontë sisters goes to show. This coincided with a point in time at which I believe it happened to be peculiarly easy to write verse. The disciplined and regular versification of the eighteenth century and its widespread use of rather obvious rhythms, once the eighteenth-century pomposity and artificiality had been dropped, produced a poetic style which seems to have been very easy to master. The result was a great flood of emotional verse, the nature and dimensions of which can be realized by exploring the dustier shelves of any old library or by looking at old magazines. Much of it is certainly very bad, but even bad verse is significant. It can be the expression of emotion, or at least of emotionalism and it may stimulate emotion, or at least emotionalism. This will be particularly true if the words are married to the right kind of music, and as the songs and hymns of the period show, music with a high efficacy in exciting emotion was being produced in the second and third quarters of the nineteenth century.

To know what stirs men's emotions at a particular period is to know something about men's minds at that period and also perhaps about what, or who, may be able to control them. This is particularly relevant to another form of popular romanticism which might escape notice. The first half of the nineteenth century is never considered to be a very interesting period in the history of the British drama, yet the drama seemed interesting enough to contemporaries. It was in a condition to respond easily to the demands of romanticism. The old tradition of blank verse tragedy remained to be reinforced by the influence of German romantic dramatists like Kotzebue. The style of acting had possibly been affected by the need to dominate a very large auditorium like that of Drury Lane, which prepared the way for a romantic school of acting of which the most notable exponent was perhaps Edmund Kean. This school reproduced on the stage all the passion and overcharged emotion which men of that period were enjoying in the other arts. Indeed this strongly rhetorical, histrionic tradition which gratified the instincts of the more inflated forms of romanticism seems to have had an influence which extended far beyond the doors of the theatre. In the language of novels, in the language of politics, perhaps even sometimes in the language of ordinary life, the language of the romantic theatre seems at times to have had its echoes. There were even times when men and women seem to have believed that rational beings could really assume the attitudes that went with it.

Of course much of this popular romanticism is trivial in intention and result. It supplied toys for the amusement of men and women. However, the toys men choose are often an index to the working of their minds, moreover what starts as a toy may in the course of time become something of deeper import. Though all through the eighteenth century there were scholars who took a serious interest in the Middle Ages there were a great many people who used medievalism as a toy. Horace Walpole played with it in his novel *The Castle of Otranto,* in the design of his house at Strawberry Hill and his collection of bric-à-brac. Others were playing the same game. The result was a certain amount of highly flavoured literature and such things as Gothic follies and other buildings in a style which was often charming but always archaeologically impossible. They were in this in sharp contrast with the buildings in the Gothic style produced in the middle of the nineteenth century, particularly with the innumerable churches in the early English style which are very often singularly lifeless and dull, but, for what that was worth, often also more accurate attempts to reproduce possible medieval originals than anything produced in the eighteenth century. The interest in the Middle Ages had survived the first period of fantasy and had deepened and become better instructed. It had inspired a good deal of serious antiquarian and historical research, and as a result mid-nineteenth-century essays in medievalism normally had more effective scholarship behind them than was the case with much that was produced in the eighteenth century.

This was even true of the novels and short stories. Even the silliest of them seem to be by several hands' breadths nearer a possible reality than the earlier romances, and such efforts as the historical novels of Charlotte M. Yonge, Charles Reade's *Cloister and the Hearth* and Charles Kingsley's *Hereward the Wake* were the respectable results of conscientious research. Serious artists and poets studied medieval models carefully and used them in their work, and so, as I have said, did architects. But they did not use Gothic styles only for churches, they adapted them to rather surprising purposes and filled the streets with Gothic railway stations and hotels, Gothic municipal offices and public libraries, Gothic factories and warehouses.

Much of this was the result of a cumbrous and not very intelligent fashion. It was whim reinforced, and in the end sometimes overweighted, by scholarship and pedantry, which had as its result the engaging but highly unsuccessful attempt of the industrialized and progressive nineteenth century to get into fancy dress. But there was more in it than that. Even the desire for fancy dress was significant and this fancy dress suggested, sometimes consciously, sometimes dimly and instinctively, values and qualities of which many men in the nineteenth century felt a need.

What they were can be best seen by looking at *Contrasts* by Pugin the architect, published in 1836. In the pictures in that book Pugin compares the splendid buildings of the Middle Ages with the mean and sordid erections in a debased classical style which filled a nineteenth-century town. Nor does he compare only buildings, for he contrasts the miserable institutions provided for the nineteenth-century poor with a highly idealized picture of almsgiving in a pre-Reformation England. It need hardly be said that Pugin's view of the Middle Ages is not historically defensible. His view of the Middle Ages, in so far as it represented past history at all, was the Middle Ages with the dirt, cruelty and corruption left out, while his view of the nineteenth century had the dirt, cruelty and corruption scrupulously left in, and emphasized. Nevertheless his criticism of the nineteenth century was valid and important, and it appealed to his imagination as intensely as it did, because he felt he had the values of earlier centuries with which to compare those of his own.

The Middle Ages, therefore, did not only attract because they provided a playground very different from the workaday world of the nineteenth century, but also because they presented a challenge. They presented this challenge to different groups with different degrees of self-consciousness and sophistication, varying from serious artists like the Pre-Raphaelite Brotherhood, or Churchmen anxiously considering the claims and potentialities of medieval Catholicism, to boys and girls who dreamed through tales of chivalry, or Nonconformist builders of chapels who felt, profoundly but vaguely, that Gothic architecture was 'Christian' whereas eighteenth-century classical architecture was not. But basically the challenge, and the attraction, were the same for all. In the past there had been an age of faith when Christianity had penetrated society as it did not do in the nineteenth century. In that age values had been honoured and principles accepted which the bustling, shoddy, utilitarian nineteenth century set at nought. Perhaps something had been lost at the Reformation, certainly something was missing from the eighteenth century, something which very many men and women longed to recover, without always clearly knowing what it was.

The obvious response to this challenge was the Catholic revival in the Anglican and Roman Catholic Churches. Pugin was an eager convert to Roman Catholicism. But the challenge was not only religious, it was also artistic and it was social, the impact of both often being the same, for the sordid ugliness which the nineteenth century so often produced seemed to those who were sensitive to it to symbolize the badness of its social principles. Indeed the social challenge came early. It is present in Southey's *Colloquies*, the extravagances of Young England, while in Disraeli's novels *Sybil* and *Coningsby,* there is reflected a kind of medievalism which is made the vehicle of social ideas. Both artistic and social challenge are present in the thought of William Morris, and most influential of all, John Ruskin turned in the 1860s from a life time largely devoted to the study of medieval Italian art to attack what seemed to him the aesthetic and moral squalor of his own day.

The results of all this were fully important. Artistically they were not always fortunate, for this impulse encouraged a literary approach to aesthetic problems. But the spiritual value was great: men and women had been encouraged to take up a position outside their own day and age and thus were enabled to take an oblique view on to their own world and to see what otherwise they might not have seen. It mattered little if this vantage point had at first only been assumed for the sheer pleasure of being outside the tedious bounds of ordinary existence. Nor did it matter if the position taken up was sometimes conceived in terms which had no relation to any history that ever really happened. What did matter was that men had been enabled to look on the world in which they lived from the outside.

But if this by-product of romanticism is important, the general importance of the tide of emotionalism it released is greater. It is not possible to read some romantic literature without either amusement or acute discomfort, yet what makes us laugh or shudder may have taught contemporaries to feel, as it was necessary that they should be taught to feel in the callous world which they had inherited from the past. The sensibility which led men to take pleasure in the more emotional parts of Dickens also prepared men to accept the social doctrine he preached. Romantic emotionalism, whatever its defects, gave vision and also gave power, and these facts are nowhere more evident and important than in the history of religion in the later eighteenth, and in the nineteenth century.

The history of religion is in this period a close parallel to the history of literature and art. Orthodox eighteenth-century religion had been more sincere than we are sometimes tempted to believe. But it had its limitations. It was moderate and sensible, it placed perhaps too great an emphasis on practical morality and based its claims for acceptance on reasoned argument.

Such argument you can find at its best in Bishop Butler's *Analogy*, which was aimed at bringing conviction to men and women wavering on the edge of deism by an appeal to the sound, but perhaps not wildly exciting, principle of probability. Such argument might convince but did not necessarily satisfy. It is, I think, true of religious history in general that an argued case never carries men very far. It may break down obstacles in the way of belief, it may confirm the already convinced; but religious faith is normally based on something of greater emotional force than reason. Men do not want to be convinced, they want to be saved; and salvation was precisely what the early Evangelical preachers, John Wesley, Whitefield and the rest, offered them.

It was salvation won through deep emotional experiences according to a prescribed plan—conviction of sin, surrender, conversion and then salvation. It was from the effects of those experiences that the Evangelical movement drew its power, whether within the Church of England or without, whether Arminian under the influence of Wesley, or Calvinist under the influence of Whitefield. Indeed how immaterial these differences are can be seen in the emotional power and general use of two hymns written by clergymen of the Church of England in the eighteenth century. 'Jesu Lover of My Soul' written by Charles Wesley and published in 1740, which is Arminian, and 'Rock of Ages' written by A. M. Toplady and published in 1775, which is Calvinist. Both were used indiscriminately by Evangelicals of all denominations and all theological opinions.

It is possible that the break came earlier in the history of religion than it did in the history of literature, and was more dramatic. But the process was the same. The heart of man had craved for something different from the commonplace it was receiving, and had got it. Man's imagination, his intuitive and visionary powers had shown him things which neither reason, nor the dutiful practice of morality, nor yet the principle of probability, could have disclosed to him. From this experience was engendered a movement which helped to revolutionize the life of England. It led to the renewal of serious religion in all classes. It played its part in the revival of the Church of England from the squalor in which many centuries of uncorrected abuse had left it, and the deadness into which it slipped in a century of religious common sense. It called into existence what was after the Church of England the largest religious body in the country, the Methodists of the old connection, and with them the various splinter bodies of Methodists, those of the new connection, the Bible Christians and the Primitive Methodists, who are important as a largely working class sect. It energized the old seventeenth-century Nonconformist bodies, the Congregationalists and the Baptists, and created a large number of other bodies, like the Brethren, which it would be difficult to categorize, as a by-product, and it is important to remember it was a by-product, it inspired the men who led the crusade against the slave-trade and slavery, it was the mainstay of Lord Shaftesbury and others who fought for the protection of factory children and chimney sweeps and for the proper treatment of lunatics. By giving life and force to the dissidence of Dissent it gave its characteristic shape to the British Liberal party. If it started in the eighteenth century, it renewed its force throughout the nineteenth century, so that it continued to provide men to try to evangelize the millions who poured into the world as the result of the population explosion.

Here is the force of romanticism. It is interesting to realize how close were the sources of this movement to the sources which fed secular popular romanticism. The same improvements of the printing-press as produced novels, magazines and books of poetry in their myriads also produced tracts, religious journals and above all hymn books. The great romantic actors Kean and Macready had as their counterparts the great Evangelical preachers, indeed their style seems to have been much the same. The emotional poetry could be directed to religious purposes as easily as to the description of secular feelings. Indeed there were many poets who did both, not only was James Montgomery in his better poetic moments a hymn writer, but H. F. Lyte who wrote 'Abide with Me', and Mrs Adams who wrote 'Nearer my God to Thee', also wrote minor romantic secular poetry.

It is, however, not for nothing that the hymns of these writers seem to have greater force and artistic truth than their secular poems. The emotion which they tried to convey not only claimed to have a profounder import, but was more likely to be based on experience that was real and not factitious. It is true that the tunes, often based on German models, which brought them home to the hearts of many men and women, are not to our taste, but it is necessary to understand their impact. Indeed if the Evangelical revival is to be understood, not as a dead historical factor to be enumerated with others in history books and ascribed with unthinking facility to purely economic causes, but as the moving living thing with power of its own, which it was, it is best to turn to its hymns, such hymns as I have named, and others particularly perhaps 'Just as I am', which was often sung at revivalist meetings. Then indeed it is a little easier to appreciate what was moving the waters.

Yet for all its force and reality it shared the inherent weakness of all romanticism, the tendency to value emotion for the sake of emotion. It is easy when you have come to value an emotion because it reveals to you a truth outside yourself to come to believe that what is important is that you should entertain the appropriate emotion, and not that you should see the truth it claims to disclose. In secular romanticism there is the tendency to concentrate on the excitement and the agony of being in love rather than on the beloved, and in religion there is the tendency to concentrate on the experiences of conversion rather than on the God to whom that experience should have led. The point is put clearly in the *Lectures on Justification* which Newman published in 1838. He says of many people at that time: 'They rather aim at experience within, than at Him that is without. They are led to enlarge on the signs of conversion, the variations of their feelings, their aspirations and longing and to tell all this to others.'

This weakness brought another with it. If experience was all-important then the work of the intellect and the business of scholarship were of little account, indeed they were suspect for they might appear to challenge the rigid theory of Biblical inspiration in which Evangelicals had immured themselves. This hardly affected the Evangelical appeal to millions of people to whom learning and the life of the mind meant little, but it meant that Evangelical Christianity became increasingly unattractive to the intelligent and educated. One of the important facts in the nineteenth century went forward. The men of light

and leading might well have been Evangelicals in the days of
Wilberforce, but they were more likely to have been drawn into
the Oxford Movement or the Catholic revival by the middle of
the century, or to have become broad Churchmen, if they retained any Christianity at all. This in turn meant that Evangelicals became less flexible, more fanatical and more apt to
persecute, and so even less attractive to very many people.

But there were greater difficulties to come. Towards the end
of the century it was becoming necessary for every Church or
religious party to adjust its beliefs to conform to the findings of
nineteenth-century science and scholarship, and the fundamen-
talist position which the Evangelicals had taken up made it more
difficult for them than for any other religious body to accept this
challenge, or to evade it. Meanwhile the springs of their power
were starting to dry up. All nineteenth-century religious movements had drawn on the reservoirs of nineteenth-century emotionalism for part of their force, indeed some of the hymns of
F. W. Faber, first a high Anglican and then a Roman Catholic,
had been as unrestrainedly emotional as those of any Protestant
revivalist. But for the Evangelicals religious emotion had been
uniquely important and they had depended more completely
than any other religious group on the techniques of revivalism.
Now those resources were going to diminish. In the last quarter
of the nineteenth century the tide began to turn, the reaction
against romanticism began. If one generation had discovered
that the intellectual methods of its predecessors had been restricted, dry and prosy, that they had refused the insights which
feeling and imagination might have given them, a later generation was to find that what had moved their parents and grand-
parents was inflated, insincere and, if not disgusting, at least
absurd.

This deflation was going to penetrate very deeply into the
whole of life. Not only was it going to deflate the forces which
had supported religion, it would also affect morality. Romanticism had been responsible for the form which much nineteenth-
century popular morality had adopted and the language in which
it had been expressed. It was very vulnerable. If it had made
men sensitive it had also led to a morbid, over-dramatized view
of sex, and also to the use of those inflated half meaningless

phrases at which later satirists have found it so easy to mock. Romanticism had also entered politics. In nineteenth-century politics the spoken word eloquently produced, played a greater part than it does now, and there was an interesting affinity between what was said on the nineteenth-century platform and what was said on the early nineteenth-century stage. The oratory of some of the Chartists such as Harney, or of some of the Young Ireland group, such as Meagher 'of the sword', is very close in its methods and its vocabulary to the tremendous speeches which were thundered out nightly at Covent Garden or at Drury Lane. Indeed in one case there is a personal link. Richard Lalor Sheil was in the 1830s after O'Connell the most eloquent orator among the Irish in the House of Commons, he was also the author of stirring blank verse dramas, such as the *Apostate*, *Bellamira* and *Evadne*, which gave the appropriate actors all the opportunities they could desire.

All this was to be punctured and to subside. By the twentieth century the methods of religious revivalism had ceased to be efficacious, except perhaps in the Highlands of Scotland and in Wales. The old methods of acting were gradually repudiated as 'Ham', and it is said that nowadays you can only hear the old style of political speech in a southern Irish country election, or some parts of the southern States of the United States. And long before the nineteenth century was over its emotional commonplaces were being put to ridicule. They were mocked at by W. S. Gilbert. Oscar Wilde amused himself with them. Samuel Butler attacked them, and in many cases Bernard Shaw or Lytton Strachey gave the *coup de grâce*. So the way was prepared for a period in which the presiding spirit seems so often to be the spirit that denies.

It is, however, impossible to take the rhetoric completely out of politics. The style may change, but the need to persuade men and to win their hearts is likely to remain or recur, and with Lloyd George and Winston Churchill to come it would be obviously absurd to say that rhetoric departed from British politics with the nineteenth century. Where there is rhetoric, there is likely to be romanticism, that is, some conception or objective commended as much by emotion as by reason. It is therefore significant that the most important legacy of romanticism to the

modern world lies in the field of politics. It is the romantic conception of nationality.

As has been said, the idea that a period of history had special
characteristics which divided it from other periods is part of the
romantic legacy to history to which Sir Walter Scott made his
great contribution. If, however, romantic sensibility could disclose what was idiosyncratic in a period, it might also suggest
that there was something idiosyncratic in the life of a nation
which could be only understood by entering into the feelings and history of the people involved, and could never be
realized by ordinary imperceptive common sense.

There is an important truth in this, but it can lead on to a
dangerous type of myth which romanticism was peculiarly likely
to generate. The nation was not seen as something unique created by the forces of history, but as something which existed before
the forces of history operated on it or at least before it was subject to the forces of recorded history. It was also something over
which the forces of history had no power. This might lead to a
mystical conception of the race or the folk taking the place of
the conception of the nation, and might make considerable use
of the kind of biological nonsense about the permanent difference of human types which was peculiarly rife in the last years
of the nineteenth and the first years of the twentieth century.
But the myths of race did not have to wait till the post-Dar-
winian period—romanticism and the real scholarship which it
often encouraged, and exploited, prepared a rich seed bed in
which the conception of race could grow. The interest in folk
lore and fairytale, the interest in old ballads, the interest in
philology and the early history of language all helped to create
a shadowy world of remote antiquity, in which a race could be
discovered and from which it could emerge to meet with heroic
constancy the vicissitudes which history would inflict upon it.

This notion combined with the romantic conception of nationality. That idea can be perhaps best seen in the work of the
great romantic historian Michelet, though much that was written in England about the Saxons and the peculiar virtues which
they were believed to have bequeathed to the Anglo-Saxons
should come into this category. That myth, however, had a
longish history behind it which stretched back into ages before

one can conveniently talk of romanticism, for it derived at least in part from seventeenth-century speculations about the Saxon origin of English Parliamentary institutions and a better example of the myth of a nationality first taking shape in the study of folk lore and ballads, and then developing into an important historical concept is probably to be found in the history of German nationalism, where the work of Herder and the brothers Grimm was used by historians like Fichte to create something very formidable indeed.

I believe that in the history of the nationalisms of most of the resurgent races of eastern Europe there is the same combination of the study of ancient story and ballad, the recital of more recent history, and passions excited by the contemporary situation all fused into a conception of great emotive force, which came to play an increasingly dominant part in politics. But there is an example much nearer home. The experiences of the Irish nation from the sixteenth or seventeenth centuries had given them good reason to develop a national self-consciousness as bitter and as passionate as that of any nation in Eurpoe, but they too learned to look back for confirmation of their unique national identity to a much more remote past. In the first half of the nineteenth century there was much interest in Irish antiquities. There were the strange speculations of Henry O'Brien, who wrote on *The Round Towers of Ireland,* and there were the folk lore collections of T. Crofton Croker. This interest was reflected in Tom Moore's Irish Songs such as 'The harp that once through Tara's Halls' and 'Avenging and bright': It is reflected in the ballads published by Gavan Duffy in the *Spirit of the Nation* in 1843 at the time of the Young Ireland movement, and the same feeling for a remote past reappeared in the studies of the Gaelic League and in Sinn Fein, having at its disposal better scholarship and not a whit less fire. It was needed to endorse the passionate determination of many of the Irish to be uniquely themselves and free from any foreign bond or influence whatsoever.

Perhaps the strangest example of the romantic view of history helping to confirm a conception of nationhood was in the southern States of the United States, for here there was in effect no real historical tradition to look back to. Nevertheless the gentlemen of the south became so obsessed with the idea that they represented an ancient chivalry that Mark Twain placed among the causes of the Civil War the works of Sir Walter Scott. It is probable, however, that the historical truth of the picture of the past on which the national legend was held to rest was im-material, in fact the realism of modern scholarship has vap-ourized several of the heroes and disintegrated many of the legends which were used to feed national myths. What mattered was that there should be an adaptation of history which could join together common feelings about the present, and exciting stories about the grandeur, heroism and tragedy of what could be held to have happened in the past into one significant whole. When this fermented in men's minds it enabled them to find themselves in a national struggle in which their own claims for freedom, for justice, for self-respect all found expression.

Thus was created what proved to be one of the most important agents in nineteenth-century history, and one of its most preg-nant legacies to the twentieth. It cannot be said that the nine-teenth century invented the sense of nationality; some such sense about the group in which a man lives probably naturally develops in most ordinary conditions of life and probably goes back in some form to the beginning of man's conscious exist-ence. But it consolidated it in many cases into an effective myth and gave an overriding moral force to its claims which it has not lost. Indeed it has extended the area in which it is effective far beyond the bounds of Europe. It seems probable that it is the strongest thing in the world today, stronger than class loy-alty internationally conceived.

Next time I will deal with another legacy of the nineteenth century which I suppose had best be called the 'Modern State'.

Altick, R. D., *The English Common Reader: A Social History of the Mass Reading Public, 1800-1900.* Chicago, 1957.
Buckley, J. H., *The Victorian Temper: A Study in Literary Culture.* London, 1952.
Clark, G. S. R. Kitson, 'The Romantic Element, 1830-1850', *Studies in Social History,* ed. J. H. Plumb, London, 1955.

Leavis, Q. D., *Fiction and the Reading Public.* London, 1932, 1965.

Webb, R. K., *The English Working Class Reader, 1790-1848: Literacy and Social Tension.* London, 1955.

8

THE MODERN STATE

I SPOKE BEFORE of one of the most formidable legacies bequeathed by the nineteenth and twentieth centuries, the idea of nationalism. In this I wish to turn to another, an equally formidable, legacy, the modern omnicompetent state into whose hands have been committed so extensive a control over the resources of the community and such great power over the men and women who compose it.

There is, however, a difference between the ways in which England has accepted these two legacies. Though in the nineteenth century English nationalism was reasonably strident, after 1918 it has been covert, in reserve and either inarticulate or developed in so sophisticated a way that it is difficult to identify. In this England is to be contrasted with Wales and Scotland, both of whom have developed movements in the twentieth century which correspond to the ordinary forms of nationalism. On the other hand the development of the state in Britain in the twentieth century has been as marked and as formidable as in any State not expressly totalitarian, although in the nineteenth century this development was so imperceptible that for most of the time no one seems to have realized what was happening.

How effective were the powers of the state in twentieth-century Britain can be seen in the two World Wars 1914-18 and 1939-45. These were total wars. In each of them each of the great States involved—France, Britain, Germany, Russia and to a less exacting extent the United States—had to place the entire resources of the community at the disposal of the government. It was a severe test for the machinery of any State, and it might have been thought that France with its Napoleonic tradition, or Germany with its Prussian tradition, would have been able to meet it more effectively than Britain with its tradition of personal independence and light government. Yet this was not so. Even in 1914-18, when Britain had to venture for the first time into the untried paths of the direct control of a large sector

126

of industry, of food rationing and universal conscription after the modern continental manner, she proved herself to be as capable of mobilizing her resources to the full as any of the other belligerents. Indeed, in one matter British organization seems to have been more effective than the corresponding German organization, with probably decisive results.

This was in the provision and distribution of food. Before 1914, as far as food was concerned, Germany seems to have been largely self-supporting, while Britain had to import a large proportion of what she needed over long and vulnerable sea routes. Yet in 1918 Germany was, at least in part, brought to her knees by hunger and malnutrition, but Britain, though she suffered discomfort, never approached real starvation and was nowhere near to being defeated by it. It is true that the grip of the British fleet on German supplies was very tight, but in 1916, 1917 and 1918 the attacks by German submarines on shipping moving inwards to the British Isles were also formidable, and the food coming to Britain had to compete for shipping space with munitions, oil and troops. Certainly in Germany the organization of the supply of food presented difficulties not present in Britain. It was no doubt easier to control the distribution of food in a country where most of it was being imported through relatively few channels than in one where it was being grown over a large area. When Germany mobilized in 1914 she took too many workers from her agriculture to allow it to maintain sufficient production for her needs during a long war. Britain's conscription came later and did not have such serious results. Nevertheless when everything is taken into account the fact remains that in this vital matter Britain was better able than Germany to organize and impose on herself a rigid state of discipline.

In the war of 1939-45 the contrast seems to be at least as marked. Comparisons are difficult, but it would certainly seem that on the whole Britain was able to devote the whole of her national resources and all the services of her men and women more effectively to the purposes of the war than Nazi Germany. Yet in the nineteenth century Germany, or at least Prussia, was known to be the most carefully organized and severely disciplined State in Europe, and of all States not barbarous Britain was supposed to be the least amenable to government control. British people were notoriously independent. They were known to be determined to keep down the powers of the executive to a minimum and to hold in detestation the endless petty interferences of continental officialdom. Where action was necessary they were anxious to do as much as possible by means of volunteers. In many matters they were prepared for things to take their own course. In Britain the police were noticeably polite, at least to the tolerably well-dressed. In Britain there was no military conscription, and before 1914 conscription in Britain seemed to be an impossibility. Certainly in the shadowed years before 1914 there were those who had begun to doubt whether a country could be safely run on those principles in the dangerous, competitive Europe that had taken shape. But, before 1914, no one would have doubted for one moment that, if it did come to a point when the survival of either nation depended on its capacity to organize itself down to the last hen-coop and the last loaf of bread, Germany would survive and Britain would not. Yet precisely the opposite happened.

The matter is the more remarkable because the independence of the ordinary Briton was not regarded by the British themselves as a matter of chance, or a failure of organization. On the contrary it was the point on which they had most prided themselves. Freedom was deemed to be the most important legacy of British history. It was believed that in Britain an individual, protected as he was by the common law, by trial by jury, by the Parliamentary system—as also by the idiosyncracies of the national character—was safer from the intrusions of authority than anyone in Germany, France or any other continental State. This pride was not new, it had received exuberant expression in the eighteenth century: 'The nations not so blessed as thee must in their turn, to tyrants fall, while thou shalt flourish great and free, the dread and envy of them all. Rule Britannia, Britannia rules the waves, Britons never', etc., or as Blackstone said in graver tones in his *Commentaries on the Laws of England:* 'The idea and practice of this political or civil liberty flourish in their highest vigour in these kingdoms, where it falls little short of perfection, and can only be lost or destroyed by the folly or demerits of its owner; the legislature, and of course the laws of

England, being peculiarly adapted to the preservation of this inestimable blessing even in the meanest subject. Very different from the modern constitutions of other States on the continent of Europe, and from the genius of the imperial law.'

These are proud words and the institutions of Great Britain in Blackstone's day did not entirely bear him out. The fleet that ensured that Britons should not be slaves was recruited by the press-gang and disciplined by the lash. The legislature which possessed such solicitude for the preservation of this inestimable blessing had passed a number of laws to ensure that many of the meanest subjects could be hanged or transported for actions of the utmost triviality. The law which Blackstone celebrated was in many respects an obsolete and artificial system in which a man could get so inextricably and expensively entangled that he passed the evening of his days in a debtors' prison. Yet Blackstone's claim was by no means wholly absurd. The danger of arbitrary arrest and imprisonment without trial was on the whole absent in England. An accused person was probably better protected in England than anywhere in the continent, as was also, in all probability, an opponent of the government. Freedom of expression was probably greater in Britain than anywhere except in Holland, and the toleration of divergent religious opinions greater than anywhere except in Holland and Prussia. Corrupt and oligarchical as it was, the British Parliamentary system was much nearer to self-government than was the constitution of any of the monarchies of contemporary Europe.

What the eighteenth century transmitted the nineteenth century improved and widened. Freedom broadened down from precedent to precedent. The press-gang fell into disuse. Law was reformed, freedom of contract secured. Innumerable unfair restrictions on poor people were removed and taxation was reduced so that they might be free to spend as much as possible of their substance as they pleased. All this was endorsed by a body of contemporary thought and prejudice which was partly economic theory, partly a system of morality and partly a political attitude endorsed by a natural suspicion of aristocratic government. Trade should be freed partly because that was the best policy, and partly because it was right to free it. Self-help should be encouraged partly because it encouraged useful enterprise, but also partly because it was morally healthy. Interference by the State should be eschewed partly because it was likely to make for expense and inefficiency, partly because it would certainly be used for jobbery and also because it was an unwarranted interference with private lives.

Yet from 1830 onwards a formidable governmental machine was being created in Britain which brought much of the conduct of life and the use of property under the control of the state, and provided precedents for more extensive controls when the time of need came. It came into existence before the necessities of the twentieth century had revealed themselves. It is sometimes believed that it came into existence as an answer to the exigent demands of a democratized electorate, but in fact it had begun effectively to develop before, in some cases long before, the Reform Act of 1867 and during the period of aristocratic preponderance. It also came into existence while the old ideas of the importance of freedom and self-help still predominated in the minds of most men. Why, then, did this happen? And how did it happen?

I believe the answer to the first question lies very largely not in the realm of theory but in that of fact. From 1830 onwards, indeed from before 1830, Britain had to suffer the results of the industrial revolution and the population explosion. She confronted the conditions which developed with a conscience made sensitive by the workings of the humanitarian movement and the religious revival which had begun in the eighteenth century. This meant she had to undertake a number of tasks which only the public power could tackle. Towns of a size never known in the country before had to be cleansed and policed and supplied with water. The public behaviour of industry had to be disciplined in the interests of those who were its neighbours, the hours of women and children in mill and mine had to be limited and the conditions under which even adult men laboured had to be controlled. At some time the myriads of children who had come swarming into the world would have to be educated. If these tasks were neglected not only would oppression and misery result but disease and social danger would inevitably follow in their train, and from time to time political disorders and epidemics such as cholera, smallpox or a variety of fevers served as timely reminders of those two disagreeable possibilities.

This, however, raises further questions. In what way did these facts make their impact on the body politic? How were these necessities perceived? Before, however, these questions can be answered the second of my original questions must be faced. How did these new powers come into existence?

The legal answer to that question is simple, for in one respect the British constitution is simple. There are in Britain no reserved subjects which an ordinary law cannot touch. A law which has been passed in the ordinary way by both Houses of Parliament and has received the Royal Assent has, as far as the King's subjects in Britain are concerned, illimitable power. It may destroy the most sacred liberties, it may demolish the most ancient privileges and it may do these things if passed, without notice, in an afternoon. It may be as immoral as the most wicked reactionary would desire or as silly as the most idealistic philosopher would wish, but if it has been passed by Parliament and assented to by the Crown it will still be the law. The judges will have to enforce it, and, if it grants to any individual or institution a discretion to take certain actions or to make regulations on certain subjects, the judges will have to endorse that discretion, except perhaps when there have been certain gross improprieties in its use. However august are the English law courts, however great their solicitude for the liberty of the meanest subject, their flank can always be turned by statute law.

This has been unquestioned since the seventeenth century, but its implications were not feared. It was felt that the British attachment to freedom and the British Parliamentary system sufficed to prevent any attack on basic liberties, and for those liberties the common law as administered by the ordinary law courts was an adequate protection. Indeed the great jurist A. V. Dicey, in his important book the *Introduction to the Study of the Law of the Constitution,* published in 1885, argued that the ordinary courts in England gave better protection to the ordinary individual than the *Conseil d'État* in France, a tribunal which specialized in conflicts which arose from the use of the public power. Dicey's view has not been confirmed by those who have studied the subject since his day.

Machinery of sufficient power to create the most potent engine of state was therefore available. The question is who was to put it in motion? Presumably the orthodox answer to that question today would be that ministers would pass legislation to implement the mandate which they had received at a general election. Even today that answer does not ring very true. What may be promised in the heat of an election may be rather different from what can be passed into law after it has been subjected to the cold light of reality and the professional advice of the civil service; while much important legislation is on matters so technical that it is unlikely ever to have been the subject of public controversy. Before 1867 this answer has even less reality. If it is to be justified, an idea of democracy must be accepted which endorses the use of the House of Commons simply as an instrument to give authority to what is alleged to be the will of the people. But before 1867 neither this, nor any other, conception of democracy was generally accepted. Also, if this conception is to be practicable, the government must be able to by-pass the independent views of members of the House of Commons. But this few governments before 1867 could be certain of doing, particularly after the repeal of the Corn Laws had worked confusion in the party system.

Moreover, there lingered on into the nineteenth century the memory of an earlier theory of the constitution which suggested that in many matters the initiative ought to rest not with ministers but with the members of either House of Parliament. Parliament, it was held, was the great inquest of the nation. It was the duty of members of Parliament to consider what was wrong in the nation. Grievances could be brought before Parliament by petition and it was in the power of either House to appoint committees to investigate anything that appeared to need investigation. If anything had to be set right it was for members of Parliament to promote the legislation to remedy it. This was not the task of ministers. It was their duty to provide the funds and promote the laws that were needed to enable the King's government to be carried on.

Probably even during the eighteenth century this division of function was not consistently observed. Certainly from the days of the younger Pitt onwards the work of governments became more all-embracing and government initiative more important. But the old view lingered on at the back of men's minds and the practice it favoured corresponded with the political realities of the middle of the nineteenth century.

For this reason the initiative in social policy was not necessarily taken by ministries acting as ministries. It might be taken by individual ministers acting to a large extent on their own or by members of Parliament who were not ministers, for it was open to any member to get a select committee appointed, or to propose a Bill on any subject that interested him. It is, for instance, significant that the movement for the protection of factory children which led to the Factory Act of 1833, always held to begin the creation of the new state, was sponsored from outside the government; its main sponsors in the early 1830s, Michael Sadler and Lord Ashley, later Lord Shaftesbury, were in fact in opposition. This situation did not change rapidly; from the days of Ashley in the 1830s to those of Samuel Plimsoll and Sir John Lubbock in the 1870s and later, a very great deal of important social policy was developed not on the initiative of governments but of individual members of Parliament.

To anyone whose ideas have been formed in modern conditions this raises an obvious question: how did such men recruit enough force to turn their Bills into law? How did they pass their Bills through Parliament without the support of a disciplined majority to back them? How did they organize sufficient support in the country without the aid of a regular political party?

As far as Parliament was concerned a private member would have to rely to a large extent on his personal authority, his powers of persuasion and the strength of his case. At least till the end of the third quarter of the nineteenth century these members might be more likely to pass a measure into law without the backing of government than they would be now. There were more confessedly independent members of the House of Commons ready to be convinced by a speech and party discipline was less exacting, so that the case for a measure which was not sponsored by the leaders of either party was more likely to be judged on its merits. Moreover the government claimed less of the time of the House and a private member's Bill had a better chance of gaining enough time to pass through all its stages into law. And there might be effective support from outside the House, for Parliament was sensitive to the pressure of public opinion.

This pressure could develop in a variety of ways. A scandal might break in the newspapers which caused public excitement, and a popular demand for redress might develop which would be taken up by members of Parliament. Or an individual might react violently when he came across conditions which seemed to him to be intolerable, as did Richard Oastler when he realized the hours of labour of the children in the mills and the conditions under which they worked. From that reaction developed the popular movement for factory reform in the West Riding, which not only commissioned Sadler and Shaftesbury but helped to keep up pressure on Parliament and on public opinion till the Ten Hours Bill was passed. But the need for reform might also be realized by more professional and systematic observers, whose techniques for advocating reform were necessarily different from those of the journalist or the popular agitator.

The most important single group among these élite reformers were undoubtedly the medical practitioners. There were by 1830 a good many medical men, often trained in Edinburgh and Glasgow, scattered about the country, and among these there were not a few who studied systematically the social conditions of the people among whom they worked and could unite to produce a very influential body of opinion indeed. There were others, not doctors, who took a systematic interest in social problems, as for instance the members of the statistical societies, or of the Social Science Association, and there was what can only be called the philanthropic élite, the people—Anglican, Quaker and very frequently Unitarian—who took a lead in social work either nationally, or, perhaps more frequently, in a particular city or district. These people were not necessarily politicians, and by no means always possessed much political power. They were not always the group which controlled the town council of the city in which they lived, or supplied the local members of Parliament, but they were often respected and devoted members of the community, they were often intelligent people, and their importance was considerable.

The favourite instrument of this type of opinion was the voluntary society, national or local, which concentrated on a particular problem or set of problems. Some of these were definitely professional, like the various medical societies such as the Epidemiological Society of London, sometimes they were purely charitable, as the Charity Organization Society was to be. The doctors and members of the charitable élite, however, often worked in close alliance and there were societies which combined both elements. This presumably was the case with the Health of Towns Association in the 1840s, or the various local sanitary societies. One élite group probably became increasingly important in the nineteenth century, the group of intelligent women who were wealthy enough to devote a good deal of leisure to systematic social work. It is significant that two of the societies who were noticeably responsible for pioneer social work after 1860 were the Ladies' Sanitary Reform Association of Manchester and Salford, founded in 1862, and the Yorkshire Ladies' Council of Education, founded in 1866.

Very often the work promoted by these groups was aimed at improving conditions in a particular district, first by voluntary work and then by moving the local authorities either to make use of an adoptive Act, or to secure the passage of a local Act for a particular purpose. Such local improvements might very well in due course be imposed by a general Act on the whole country. But action on a national scale might be attempted either through a devoted member of Parliament, or by petition. Probably the petitions of the Medical Societies were most often successful, but success in Parliament was more likely if the promoters of a measure could enlist the support of a fairly wide section of public opinion. This could be best done if the emotions of the public could be touched, possibly by the dramatic story of a catastrophe which ought to have been prevented, or the forcible account of conditions which ought no longer to be tolerated. The trouble about such movements of opinion was that they were apt to be volatile. A suitably strong stimulus could carry a measure right through Parliament, as when the revelation in 1842 of the horrible conditions that prevailed in coal-mines carried the Act of that year to deal with those conditions through both Houses of Parliament without much delay. On the other hand a burst of public feeling might support a reform eagerly and then die away when it was still needed. This is what happened in the early days of the movement for public health. The revelations in Chadwick's famous report on the sanitary condition of the working classes produced a burst of public feeling which helped Chadwick and the sanitary reformers at first very greatly. But this slackened off dangerously when the movement was exposed to virulent attack in the early 1850s.

This fluctuation of opinion was probably directly related to what was being pressed at any given moment in the newspapers, particularly *The Times*. Indeed the part played by the press, both national and provincial, is very important. Mid-nineteenth-century newspapers with their packed columns, small print and now yellowing paper, do not look very appetizing and it is difficult to remember how exciting they once were. In fact they were probably better equipped for the task of exposing scandals and working up feeling over intolerable conditions than is a modern newspaper. Much of the reporting was factual and detailed. The public was treated to, as near as possible, verbatim accounts of debates in Parliament, government enquiries, trials in court and, what were too frequently relevant, inquests on unfortunates whose fates provided a commentary on failures of public policy or local administration. Of course all this was slanted and selective. All the papers were noisily partisan. Sometimes this was the result of local politics, like the standing battle between the Liberal *Leeds Mercury* and the Tory *Leeds Intelligencer*, which was of considerable importance in developing the case for factory reform. Sometimes it was the result of the opinions of the proprietor. It was John Walter's views which led *The Times*, in the late 1830s and early 1840s, to publish in full every account that it could find of what was discreditable to the new Poor Law. Since the control was personal, a paper could change sides; the change in *The Times*'s attitude towards Chadwick from warm approval to undiscriminating hostility did as much as anything else to ruin Chadwick in the 1850s. But almost every literate person from the Queen and Prince Albert downwards must have studied some newspaper, and the methods of the newspapers, even their partisanship, were well qualified to excite people's interests, form their opinions and drag ugly facts from dark corners into the glaring light of public controversy.

The newspapers were, however, not the only source from which information was fed into debate. There were serious magazines, controversial novels, such as those by Dickens or Charles Reade, and polemical books. There were also innumerable pamphlets, as anyone will know who has ventured among the more neglected shelves of any large library. Printing was cheap and men were contentious, so that they not only indulged in the verbose hard-hitting controversies which filled the correspondence columns of the newspapers, but were apt to give their views to the public at greater length at their own expense. In addition to this there were government publications, which more people were prepared to read then than now. How influential they could be in exciting feeling can perhaps be realized from the account of William Cory, then a first year undergraduate at Cambridge, of his reading in 1842 Chadwick's *Report on the Sanitary Condition of the Labouring Classes* 'with most savage interest, some pages with my teeth clenched and my feet kicking out as if I was in a football game'. It was for this reason that the report of a select committee of either House or of a Royal Commission, when skilfully directed to a preconceived conclusion, were such admirable instruments for propaganda.

All this provided a force which could be used to create a public demand for legislation on a particular subject. The opinion so mobilized was not necessarily drawn from any particular party, or class, or religious denomination. It was not always instructed by the same political philosophy, or by any political philosophy. It could at times be wayward or wrongheaded. But it provided the force needed to attack the evils that infested the body politic.

If, however, the initiative in social policy did not necessarily lie with the government there might be circumstances which could force the development of it into government hands, and these might even secure that part of any further initiative passed to men in the government service. There is an early example of this in the history of factory legislation. When in 1833 Lord

Ashley, who had become the sponsor for factory reform, proposed the Ten Hours Bill, he met with such stubborn opposition that in the end in despair he yielded up the question to the Whig government. They, in order to settle the matter, promptly passed a measure of their own. This gave much less than the factory reformers desired, but it was a contrast to previous factory Acts in the fact that, whereas they had been inoperative, the Bill of 1833 contained a provision to make sure it came into force, for it was to be operated by four inspectors who were to have the powers of magistrates.

These inspectors would necessarily be the servants of the central government. They would be paid by the government, they would report to the government and in due course a minister of the Crown would have to be responsible for them. Their appointment was a recognition of the fact that if a social policy was to be effective government machinery would have to be created to put it into force, since it was no good trusting either to self-help or to the ordinary operations of the law, even when it had been reinforced by specially directed statutes. From this fact springs the development of a great deal of the machinery of the modern state. As a matter of fact these inspectors were not quite the first examples of this development, but it is convenient to start with them. They are an obvious precedent for much that was to come and they are also an example of another factor which was to be of considerable importance. They were instructed to meet together to concert regulations and to report. Thus was created an expert official opinion on which future administration would be based and which all future legislation must take into account; indeed many of the clauses of the next factory Act, that of 1844, were based on their recommendations.

This suggests an important possibility. Not only was the state equipping itself with officials with direct executive authority to put its commands into effect, but it was also gaining an intelligence service which would enable it to accumulate expert and professional knowledge based on experiment and experience on the subjects of social policy. This would certainly lead to future legislation based on an understanding of the deficiencies of past laws, and, more than that, the administrators themselves would become the most expert guides for the social policy of the future.

The full possibilities of this suggestion can be realized not so much by looking at the factory inspectors as at the man who invented them. When the government desired to produce a Bill on the factory question as an alternative to Ashley's they instructed Edwin Chadwick to draw it up. For Chadwick had served as one of the commissioners in an enquiry into the factory question, which had been set up as a counter to the report of the select committee which Sadler had dominated. It was Chadwick who originated the idea of inspectors to enforce the Act, and he was soon to be the author of much more important legislative and administrative developments. He had been seconded to the enquiry into the factory question from his work as one of the commissioners enquiring into the operation of the Poor Laws, and the new Poor Law of 1834 was largely based upon his ideas.

The new Poor Law was one of the most important Acts of the century. It was an effective attack on the old system of aristocratic self-government. It drastically remoulded the whole system by which poor relief was administered. The parishes, which had handled poor relief since the Elizabethan Poor Law was established, were combined into unions governed by elective Boards of Guardians. The control of the Poor Law by the justices of the peace and the right of the justices to order poor relief was taken from them. In its place the unions were put under the very strict control of the Poor Law Commissioners sitting in London. They issued instructions about the principles on which relief was to be administered and even appointed the servants through whom the work was to be done. Never had a central authority claimed such power over the country since the Star Chamber was abolished.

In fact the new Poor Law was not only devised by a government servant; it gave great opportunities to government servants. The Commissioners to whom Chadwick was secretary were in a position to control the administration of poor relief. If they used their position to investigate the causes of poverty and modified their policy accordingly, their work might be the beginning of a social policy, founded on the accumulated knowledge which the government alone possessed and directed by government experts who would have a more technical grasp of the matter in hand than anyone else in the country.

If this was to be done Chadwick would seem to be of all men the man best equipped to do it. If expert government was to mean not only government based on official experience, but also government based on statistics, on careful objective enquiry and on experiment rather than on the guesses, *a priori* judgments, loose assumptions and passionate assertions, which so often provide the ordinary medium of exchange in political discussion, then Chadwick's whole past had prepared him for the task. He first distinguished himself in an enquiry into life insurance, in which he demonstrated beyond doubt that careful calculations were a better guide to actuarial probabilities than the rule of thumb assertions which most insurers used. His work, on this and on the possibilities of a preventive police, commended him to Jeremy Bentham and in the last years of Bentham's life their association was very close. It was a congenial association for Chadwick, for he shared with the master a contempt for historical values and perceptions, and a confident belief in the absolute authority of radical analysis. They both had strong authoritarian instincts. Therefore Chadwick's whole past and his natural cast of mind led him to distrust the common assumptions which men usually accepted as the basis for policy and legislation and to wish to replace them by the results of careful systematic research. Legislation which was based on such research he called 'scientific legislation', and he believed it was all-important that future legislation in Britain should be 'scientific legislation' and not like the casual guesses of the past. In this of course he was right. It was important that the developing social policy of the country should be directed by what Chadwick would no doubt call 'scientific' enquiry, and for this the amendment of the Poor Law was the right starting point. Certainly neither poverty, and still less pauperism, are the primary causes of social evils. They are not causes but results. But they are also symptoms, and in the Britain of the first half of the nineteenth century the poverty that existed everywhere, and the pauperism that most emphasized it, lead directly to the problems with which a dynamic social policy ought to deal.

In fact the major opportunity was lost. It is possible that Chadwick's measure was too dogmatically conceived and too rigidly executed. Certainly it became one of the most unpopular

laws of the century. In the long run this might not have mattered if the measure had been a starting point for a systematic
enquiry into the causes of poverty, which would have led to
their differentiation and appropriate treatment. Chadwick was
prepared to use the measure in this way, but unfortunately
Chadwick was not master of the situation. In spite of promises
made to him he did not become one of the Commissioners appointed to administer the Act, he only became their secretary.
The men who became Commissioners did not share his views.
They regarded the new Poor Law as a law to be administered,
not as an experiment to be developed, and Chadwick as their
very unruly and difficult servant. His enquiries were frowned
upon, difficulties of one sort or another reduplicated themselves
and Chadwick was in due course eliminated. As a result the
Poor Law seems to have become dead. The old attitude seems
to have prevailed that pauperism was a phenomenon to be treated
in isolation, to be relieved or discouraged according to the needs
and apparent deserts of the people who happened to be paupers,
and the Poor Law Commissioners were there to administer the
law about paupers.

Nevertheless the failure of the Poor Law Commission to take
advantage of its opportunities did not mean that all opportunities
for 'scientific legislation' were lost. If the Commissioners themselves would not take the lead in the attack on the causes of
poverty, those who were their subordinates were able to continue
their assault under other auspices. The two most obvious causes
of poverty were ignorance and disease, and in 1839 Kay-Shuttleworth, who had been an Assistant Poor Law Commissioner, became secretary of the newly created Committee of the Privy
Council on Education to fight the one; while already in 1838
Chadwick had commissioned three doctors to enquire into the
causes of epidemic diseases in the metropolis, which was to be
the beginning of his bitter battle against the other.

It is probably unnecessary to describe the splendours and
miseries of that battle, the tremendous effect on public opinion
of Chadwick's famous report in 1842, the confirmation of its
findings by a Royal Commission which was steered by Chadwick
to that end and the first Public Health Act, of 1848, which set
up the Board of Health with Chadwick as a paid commissioner.

It is a tale of both success and failure. The Act of 1848, together with local Acts passed at this time for particular localities, certainly laid the foundation of the sanitary reform without which life in increasingly crowded and urbanized Britain would have become increasingly intolerable. On the other hand the work was partial, it was possible to evade the Act, and Chadwick and the Board of Health aroused animosities so violent that in 1854 they came to a head in the House of Commons, and Chadwick was driven out of public life, and his work partially demolished.

Chadwick's story must of course be understood in its immediate personal and contemporary frame of reference. That, however, should not disguise the fact that it presents, possibly for the first time, a modern problem of permanent importance, the problem of the relation of the expert in government to the ministers, the Parliament and the electorate who are his nominal masters. It is necessarily a difficult relationship. In the last resort the expert's obedience must be to the facts revealed by his knowledge, facts which do not change with the varying fortunes of political parties at irrelevant elections, or with the different views of transitory ministers. As a result a situation may arise when either the expert must surrender his opinion at the demands of ignorant men and give his service to a policy which he knows to be wrong, and may believe to be disastrous; or alternatively ministers may have to endorse a policy which they did not support before they entered office, which they do not like, or which is too technical for them to understand and to judge.

But, though the problem is a permanent one, it is necessary, in order to understand what happened in the middle of the nineteenth century, to recognize that the constitutional setting in which this problem had to be worked out then was very different from the constitutional situation nowadays.

Nowadays the expert in government is very well protected against the violence of public controversy. He is protected by the conventions which prevent him from expressing in public his views on those controversial matters, which are the subject of his service. He is also protected by the decent myth of ministerial responsibility, by virtue of which the politician at the head of a department takes responsibility for the actions of his subordinates whether they are carrying out a policy of his own devising, or one promoted by the officials in his department. Under this dispensation if there has been a conflict about the policy to be undertaken it will have taken place behind closed doors in conditions in which an expert is likely to have had advantages which he would not have had in the forum of public discussion; in which, also, a politician is not likely to be so severely embarrassed by what he has already said in public; and in which ignorant and passionate members of the general public cannot take sides. When the policy emerges into the light of day and perhaps takes effect in legislation there will be a further protection, the protection of a disciplined majority in the House of Commons who will normally support the decisions of ministers, even if they also do not wholly like, or fully understand, them.

In the middle of the nineteenth century these protections did not exist, or only existed in rudimentary form. To begin with, governments could not then be sure of a disciplined majority in the House of Commons. This was amply proved at that black moment in 1854 when Chadwick was broken in spite of the fact that he enjoyed the support of the strongest minister in the Cabinet, Lord Palmerston. But there was no guarantee that a civil servant would be adequately supported by any minister, for between 1830 and 1870 the practice and theory of our modern doctrine of ministerial responsibility had not been fully developed. It was in fact created by the conditions that began to prevail after 1830.

The doctrine necessarily depends on there being a clear distinction between the permanent civil servant and the political minister who is responsible for him. But before 1830 that distinction if it existed was shadowy. The officials who served in the government from ministers in the Cabinet to clerks in the customs house were primarily the King's servants, all equally responsible to King, Parliament and the Law. At the top there was, it is true, a group who were essentially politicians. They might well form a group who came into office and would go out of it together and who owed a common allegiance to a leader who might be the Prime Minister. But there might be more than one group in office, and there might be ministers in the House of Commons who were really civil servants and not politicians. The line of demarcation was not clear for it was possible for a man to graduate, as did Huskisson or Herries, without any break in his career from the position of a clerk in a public office to high place as a minister of the Crown with a seat in the Cabinet. By the end of that process he would no doubt have become a member of a group of politicians and have to share their fortunes, but, if we are to accept Herries's words in 1827 at their face value, that change might be regretted. Indeed it might endanger a man's future if that group fell out of favour, as it did that of Herries in 1830.

In the years 1830-2 this was changed. With the defeat of the Duke of Wellington's government and the passing of the first Reform Bill the idea that the ministry was in a personal sense the King's government faded, and the whole ministry in Parliament became more emphatically the product of party politics. There was no longer a place in the House of Commons for relatively uncommitted civil servants. At the same time the machinery of government was expanding, new and important functions were being added to it, so that there was an increasing number of important civil servants who were without question outside politics.

Government was taking on a new shape, and to a certain extent there was developing a new constitutional theory. The government was to a greater extent than it had been before the servant of Parliament, not of the King, and therefore more completely dependent on the favour of the House of Commons. As a result the responsibility of the executive to the House of Commons for all its actions was much more marked, a fact which was emphasized in the sharp party politics of the years after the Reform Act during which the executive was attacked with a bitterness and a consistency that might not have seemed legitimate if it had still been the government of the King. This produced difficulties for the increasing number of civil servants who were not politicians, since if attacked they had no means of replying. The answer to this problem was for the government to be so organized that all important functions would be clearly covered by some political minister who could speak for the non-political civil servants in the House. However, the need to do this was not at first realized, and when new functions were needed governments continued for some time to create departments in which there was no minister to take responsibility, or in which it was not clear what minister was responsible. For instance the Poor Law Commission was not under any responsible minister, and when later the Committee of the Privy Council on Education was formed, the responsibility for its actions might be presumed to be confusedly shared among the various ministers who were its members, unless it adhered to the Lord President of the Council, whom members of the House of Commons might find rather hard to reach.

In the case of the Poor Law Commissioners the sequel made the need for Parliamentary cover abundantly obvious. As Walter Bagehot said afterwards, the House of Commons would not let the Commission alone, and in 1847 it had to be dissolved and a Parliamentary head added. Writing in 1865, Bagehot drew the right moral. 'The experiment of conducting the administration of a public department by an independent unsheltered authority has often been tried, and always failed. Parliament always poked at it, till it made it impossible.' The lesson, however, had not been fully learnt in 1847, for the next year the Board of Health was erected, and it contained a minister, two paid commissioners and an independent commissioner. The minister could therefore be outvoted. Perhaps it had been intended that the minister should be responsible, but, since one of the paid commissioners and the unpaid commissioner were such powerful characters as Chadwick and Lord Shaftesbury, there was bound to be trouble when they were given an uncongenial minister, and trouble there was.

In due course this lesson would be learnt and effective ministerial responsibility, with its sequel in effective political control, would be extended over all the various departments of the central government. It is, however, very important in the history of the development of the State in Britain that this process was not complete till towards the end of the third quarter of the century; so that during a critical period various important civil servants were not under effective political control. This independence was enhanced by the fact that clearly in the period immediately after 1830 the conventions which enjoin on civil servants' reticence on controversial matters had not yet been developed, probably because the division in the King's service was new.

There are some striking examples of this. Among the civil servants whom the Whigs appointed after 1830 were several men of force and ability, who had before appointment taken up controversial positions on matters with which they were to deal as servants of the Crown. After appointment they did not see why entry into the public service should shut their mouths or restrict what they thought it right to do. As a result things were said and done which would not have been possible today. MacGregor and Porter at the Board of Trade, touching on the most hotly controversial subject of the moment, openly advocated the doctrine of complete free trade, which the government of the day had not yet accepted, while Porter maintained close relations with the Anti-Corn Law League when that body was engaged in a furious assault on his political masters; indeed, was going so far as to call the Prime Minister a 'murderer'. Rowland Hill, a milder man, the author of the penny postage and an official in the Post Office, was prepared to use his friendship with members of Parliament outside the government to start a movement to get his immediate superior in the office, whom he felt was an obstacle to his schemes, transferred to another department or retired on a pension. And Chadwick was able to use all the publicity which he could exploit to develop an active policy in public health.

Of course he paid for his independence. Without the protection of a government majority, without the cover of ministerial responsibility, without the cloak of anonymity, an expert in the civil service is like an exposed nerve in the body politic. Chadwick's reforms and projects were known to be his, he received in full measure such praise and such abuse as they earned. The abuse was noisy and venomous and rose to a climax in 1854, when it overwhelmed him. Nevertheless from a national point of view the advantages of the position were incalculable. Chadwick's relative independence, the fact that he was able to appeal directly to public opinion, enabled the movement for public health to get started. It is difficult to see how otherwise this could have happened. If Chadwick had been enclosed in a fully organized government department speaking only through the mouth of a responsible minister, unable to use the expedients he did use to gain public support, it seems unlikely that in those days he would have accomplished very much. It was the lag in the development of the institutions of Parliamentary government that enabled the knowledge of the expert to be used for the development of social policy as it was used in the two middle quarters of the nineteenth century. When that lag came to an end there was a change and a retardation.

It was this development of social policy that led to the creation of the State as we know it nowadays in Britain. It was not the work of governments pursuing coherent policies, still less was it the legacy of any particular party or the result of the general adoption of any particular philosophy. It was the work of individuals reacting as best they might to particular problems and situations, individual ministers, individual members of Parliament, individual civil servants and individual members of the general public. Since this was so the work was piecemeal and sporadic, and for this reason not only did contemporaries not understand the significance of what was happening, but even historians writing in later times have not always realized how much was done before 1867 and to what extent what was done after 1870 was a consolidation, if also an extension, of what had been initiated earlier in the century. For this reason it may be worth-while, at the risk of being tedious, to recapitulate some of the things which were started and some of the laws which were passed.

Since the Factory Act of 1833 is usually taken as the beginning of the creation of the new state, it is probably convenient to start with the laws for the protection of labour. The law of 1833 for the protection of children and young persons in a variety of textile mills was followed by an Act of 1844 and another in 1847. This last was the much desired Ten Hours Bill. It was modified by a legal decision and evaded, and had to be strengthened by an Act of 1853, indeed, it might be said that the law did not really fulfil its purpose till the great consolidating Workshops and Factories Act of 1878. Meanwhile control was being extended, largely apparently under the impulse of the factory inspectors, to other factories connected with the manufacture of textiles, to printworks in 1847, to bleaching and dyeing works in 1860, to lace factories in 1861 and to various processes for the finishing of cloth in 1863 and 1864.

In 1842, however, the terrible conditions which Shaftesbury had revealed as existing in the mines had caused the passage of the first Act controlling conditions in that industry, followed by Acts of 1850 and 1860, and the beginning of an important controlling service of inspectors and the establishment of the School of Mines. In addition to this, in certain classes of labour there was a long tradition of protection going back to the beginning of the century or before, which was continued when other old-fashioned controls were being swept away. For instance, in 1843 a combination of the Thames Coalwhippers and the City Corporation produced a Bill to protect and decasualize this form of labour, which was taken over by Gladstone and passed into law. There was also a long history of Acts relating to seamen, including the Navigation Acts which were repealed in 1849. As, however, old measures for the protection of seamen were abandoned new measures were introduced. There were Acts in 1833 and 1835, in 1844 an important Act was passed by Sir James Graham as Home Secretary, and in 1854 the great Merchant Shipping Act was passed by Edward Cardwell as President of the Board of Trade. It aimed both at protecting seamen and ensuring safety at sea. It had 584 sections and passed so easily that Lord John Russell suspected that Cardwell must have abandoned some 'great public interest' to get it through. Other Acts followed, and still much remained to be done as the career of Plimsoll was to show.

It would be tedious to do more than mention some of the Acts which dealt with other forms of labour and which were passed in the 1860s. An Act which dealt with bakehouses was passed in 1863, with factories making earthenware, lucifer matches, percussion caps and cartridges in 1864. In 1864 also an Act dealt with chimney-sweeps, but this was one of a series of laws that had tried to deal with this subject from the eighteenth century onwards and was not itself fully effective. In 1867 a complicated Act covered a large number of industries and was accompanied by a Workshops Act. Women and children in agriculture were at last reached in 1868.

In all this the factory inspectors were all-important, and so was Shaftesbury, who throughout a long life was forever pushing enquiries into dark corners in which children were abused. Even when he finished his course much remained to be done. Indeed, looking back on the conditions in which nineteenth-century labour had to work the whole development seems painfully slow and painfully incomplete, and it has to be remembered that most of this legislation was directed to the protection of women, adolescents and children, not adult male labour, though adult males gained advantage from it. Yet viewed as a system, in its way new, coming into existence in about forty years, it is formidable and significant. It seems to be moving inevitably to that end which Dicey considered to be imminent in 1905: 'Whenever any man, woman or child renders services for payment, there in the track of the workers will appear the inspector.'

If the forces of the industrial revolution confronted the country with the problem of the hours of labour, particularly the labour of children, and the control of the condition of labour, the forces behind the population explosion combined with the forces of the industrial revolution to confront it with the problems of public health and sanitation, and the need to preserve or create some of the amenities of life in very desolate places. These necessities might press on the governors of the country at two points: on those who were concerned in local government in those districts where the results of these dynamic forces were most apparent and dangerous, and on those who were concerned with the central government whose task it might be to assist, or compel, the local authorities to do their duty. Both sides of the problem had been in evidence before 1854. There had undeniably been the need both for encouragement and even compulsion from the centre; and both had been supplied by Chadwick and the Board of Health. The element of compulsion was supplied in the Nuisance Removal and Disease Prevention Acts of 1846 and 1848 which provided powers that could be put into effect against epidemic disease, and in the section of the Public Health Act of 1848 which empowered the Board of Health to bring the Act into force in districts where the death rate rose above a certain figure. There were also the Acts of 1852 and 1853 which enabled the Privy Council to close, or control the opening of, cemeteries. And there was an Act which imposed minimal standards on the London water companies.

However, the best part of the work had been in the sphere of assistance and encouragement. Much of what had been done had had the object of facilitating the voluntary action of local authorities. The most useful part of the Health Act of 1848 was that which provided facilities for its voluntary adoption. A good many places took it up, while certain enlightened local authorities had promoted legislation to start on the work before the Act was passed and to extend their activities to deal with matters that were outside the scope of the Act. Liverpool attacked slum housing by obtaining local Acts in 1842 and 1846. Their object was to try to eliminate cellar dwellings, an object which was defeated by the vast Irish immigration that followed the potato famine. In 1843 Birkenhead, and in 1845 Nottingham took comparable powers. With the attack on bad housing went not only the provision of adequate drainage and a reasonable water supply but, even in this early period, some authorities began to go further and to supply amenities, such as parks and recreational grounds.

In this also they had the encouragement of legislation promoted by various members of Parliament. In 1841 a sum of money was provided at the instance of Silk Buckingham, a private member of the House of Commons, for the provision of recreation grounds. The Inclosure Act of 1845 prevented the inclosure of village greens and of areas within a certain distance of large towns, it also provided for the setting aside of a certain area for public recreation. In 1847 the Town Improvement Clauses Act facilitated the taking of powers to establish public parks. In 1852 a member of Parliament who had taken a particular interest in such matters, R. A. Slaney, got Parliament to pass an Act to facilitate the purchase and maintenance of recreation grounds and playgrounds. This was followed in due course by other Acts with the same object, while in 1845 William Ewart, a member of Parliament with an interest in popular education, got a measure passed to enable towns to support museums, and in 1850 to support libraries, out of the rates. This was also the beginning of much legislation on this subject. In 1846 on a rather different subject an Act was passed to empower boroughs and parishes to establish public baths and wash-houses. This was largely the result of the activities of a charitable society and the influence of a successful private experiment in Liverpool. In 1851 Lord Shaftesbury secured the passage of two Acts: one to provide for the inspection of common lodging houses and the other to enable local authorities to erect lodging houses for working men or to convert buildings for the purpose.

Many of these Acts seem to have passed without much opposition. There were moments 'when some heart indignant' broke at the idea of taking money from a man's pocket by means of the rates to spend on such objects. But in many cases they got through most of their stages without debate. The full fury of opposition was reserved for Chadwick and his colleagues on the Board of Health. This was partly inspired by what became an almost blind hatred of Chadwick, partly by a general dislike of government interference, and on its most rational side by a belief that these things ought to be handled by responsible local authorities and not be the subject of dictation from the centre.

This was in fact the belief of the men who immediately succeeded Chadwick. In 1854 Chadwick's Board of Health was temporarily replaced by a Board under a responsible minister, Sir Benjamin Hall. Hall had been the spokesman of the London vestries against Chadwick. When, however, he faced the responsibilities of his office with an epidemic of cholera beginning, Hall began to see the necessity of central control. In his most important Act, the Metropolitan Management Act of 1855, which set up the Metropolitan Board of Works and made possible the drainage of London, he took a firm line with the vestries and made them appoint Medical Officers of Health, and he began to take a more authoritarian line in the other legislation he promoted. The dislike of centralization, however, remained strong in the House of Commons and neither he, nor his successor Cowper, were able to get all the legislation they wanted through the House. Indeed, though in 1858 a very useful local government Act was passed, it was accompanied by a Public Health Act which transferred the medical oversight of the country to the Privy Council. What remained of the central Board of Health had disappeared for ever.

Such powers of the central authorities of the state over the medical matters as remained were scattered promiscuously among different offices, and in so far as there was an intelligent nucleus in the Privy Council it was reduced to the tasks of enquiry, advice and exposure. These functions, however, sufficed. Significantly, as in 1842, the next stage in the development of a policy on public health was to be promoted by exposures for which an official in the government was responsible. Dr, later Sir, John Simon became eminent as the Medical Officer of Health in the City of London, he was in the confidence of Hall and in 1855 he became Medical Officer to his reformed Board of Health. When that disappeared he became Medical Officer to the Privy Council. In that situation he could direct inspections, initiate enquiries, receive and issue reports, and his annual reports had a very important effect on the formation of educated opinion, particularly medical opinion.

Simon was a very different man from Chadwick, whom he admired, but whose mistakes he recognized. He was different in temperament and significantly different in training, for he was a doctor and worked through doctors, while Chadwick held all medical men in contempt. He had also believed, as Chadwick had never believed, that he could do what was needed through the voluntary co-operation of local authorities. Experience, however, seems to have taught him the utter inadequacy of a system which placed much reliance on such co-operation, and, particularly in his 1864 and 1865 reports, he described very clearly the disgusting conditions which still prevailed in different parts of Britain: the infamous housing conditions, particularly in country districts, the cholera-prone towns, the polluted water supplies, the piles of filth adjoining human habitations. For all this he blamed both the deficiencies of the various relevant Acts of Parliament and the discreditable failure of many of the local authorities who were supposed to administer them. The Acts did not touch many of the matters, which were now seen to be of importance in maintaining public health, they were also ambiguous at critical points and they lacked coercive power. Many of the local authorities were not only negligent and incapable, they also at times acted in collusion with those who profited by the worst nuisances.

This condemnation had its effect. In 1866 the government

proposed a Sanitary Act, which was helped through Parliament by the appearance in the country at a critical moment of timely epidemics. Under this Act, Simon said dryly, 'the grammar of common sanitary legislation acquired the novel virtue of an imperative mood'. All local authorities were to be compelled to do their duty. Once again an expert in the government service had been responsible for a major change in the policy of the state, and incidentally had led the way to the path that led to his destruction. Immediately, however, the Act of 1866 initiated the era of consolidation, which started, it is to be noted, the year before the Second Reform Bill was passed. There followed a series of Acts which imposed a general standard on the country. In 1868 W. M. Torrens, an independent Liberal member, secured a general law which imposed on the owners of all houses the duty of keeping them in reasonable repair. Between 1869 and 1871 there was a Royal Commission, the findings of which were implemented by a series of statutes culminating in the great consolidating statute of 1875.

It is from this period that an effective system of public health in Britain must be held to date, but it is important not to underestimate the significance of the earlier, more haphazard period. What was done in that period, particularly by the more enlightened local authorities, is important. If it had not been done there would have been no health service to consolidate. Even the haphazard character of that period is significant, for the whole development of British social policy is haphazard. It was at the mercy of circumstances. Particularly offensive revelations at the critical moment, the effective advocacy of a member of Parliament, a minister, a civil servant, a newspaper or a reforming group, might launch a reform. The chances of a fluid Parliamentary situation, or the inattention of potential opponents, might enable it to get under way. The fact that the evil which it was intended to cure was found to exist in closely analogous situations in the body politic might lead to the natural extension of the service which had been developed, and if the department of government on which it had been grafted was alive then the new service might grow and develop its own inherent life.

But there were cases where these conditions were not present. The initial impetus might not be sufficient. The technical knowledge which would make action possible might not be available. Serious opposition might develop. The department of government on to which the new service was grafted might itself be dead, and the new service might never come alive, and as a result of these largely accidental differences the reform of evils which seem to us equally insistent might not take place or be strangely delayed.

For instance, the philanthropic élite, particularly of the Quakers, had, even in the eighteenth century, drawn attention to the problems of the insane. This had been reinforced by intermittent revelations of the ugly things which might happen behind closed doors to people who were held to be mad. A series of laws had been passed to protect lunatics, but in 1827 a select committee of the House of Commons had unearthed facts which showed their protection was illusory, so that in 1828 Robert Gordon, who had been Chairman of the Committee, induced Parliament to pass a measure which gave the Home Secretary control over the places where lunatics were lodged. This control was to be exercised through visiting magistrates and fifteen lunacy commissioners. Lord Shaftesbury, then of course Lord Ashley, had seconded Gordon's motion. He became a very active lunacy commissioner and accumulated a good deal of knowledge on the subject, and in 1845 introduced and passed two Bills to compel the erection of asylums in counties which had not erected them and to establish a permanent lunacy commission with six paid and six unpaid members. There was, of course, more to be done and other Acts to be passed, but at least before the half century was reached a reasonable system had been developed, very largely through the advocacy of Shaftesbury. If the system remained unsatisfactory it was very largely on account of medical ignorance of the nature of, and of the proper treatment for, mental disease.

This story is to be contrasted with the miserable history of the State's failure to develop any system to secure the welfare of another class of beings just as helpless and even more important than lunatics, infants in the first years of their life. Again interest in the matter went back into the eighteenth century. Lying-in hospitals had been founded then for expectant mothers, and the Foundling hospital and a variety of orphanages had been brought into existence for unwanted children. But it seems to be in the 1860s and early 1870s that the real beginnings of the modern movement for maternity and child welfare can be traced. In 1862 the Ladies' Sanitary Reform Association of Manchester and Salford introduced health visiting at homes where a birth had taken place. In 1866 Dr Farr, the statistician in the Registrar-General's Office, asked the Obstetrical Society of London for information about the mortality of children under five years. The society appointed a committee to study the matter which included Dr Curgenven, the Secretary of the Harveian Society, a doctor deeply interested in the problem, who founded in 1870 the Infant Life Protection Society. The Committee reported back to Dr Farr in 1869, and in 1870 the Obstetrical Society formulated five 'suggestions for Legislative Enactments' for the protection of children at birth, and began to develop the scientific training of midwives. Meanwhile in 1871 the Yorkshire Ladies' Council organized lectures for mothers in Leeds and other Yorkshire towns.

At this point the stage seems set for the development of an effective policy to secure the welfare of mothers and infant children, but it did not develop. It is true that Parliament passed in 1872 the Infant Life Protection Act, but this was an Act evoked by the revelations that emerged at the trial in 1870 of Margaret Waters, a notorious baby farmer, and was only concerned with the protection of foster children. In other matters no advance was made. One of the measures suggested in 1870 was a law to secure the proper qualification and registration of midwives. This was repeatedly pressed upon Parliament, but it was opposed by doctors who, it is to be feared, did not wish certified midwives to cut into their fees. The Local Government Board was appealed to but, as will be seen, the Local Government Board with Stansfeld as minister, Lambert in control and Simon effectually cordoned off was, as far as health matters concerned, dead, and no help was given. The Bill for the registration of midwives was not passed till 1902, and then against official opposition. An adequate policy on infant and child welfare had to wait till later in the twentieth century when the pressure of the élites had become greater and there had been a change in the Board and in its political masters.

In other matters, with the right advocacy, or the right pro-
vocation, or better still with both, in the middle, or before the
middle of the nineteenth century important things were done
and important services started. The state's concern with vaccination goes back as far as 1808 when Parliament started a national
vaccine establishment. This did not achieve much, and when
the Registrar-General began to publish his returns on the causes
of death in the country it became evident that smallpox was
still a serious killing disease. The matter was taken up by the
Provincial and Medical Surgical Association, the predecessor
of the British Medical Association. They petitioned Parliament
in 1840, and Lord Ellenborough, an opposition member of the
House of Lords, but with the assent of the government, per-
suaded Parliament to pass a measure which imposed on all
Boards of Guardians the duty of providing free vaccination. It
also placed the whole matter under the control of the Poor Law
Commission and forbade the dangerous practice of innoculation.
This produced some improvement, but still the number of
deaths from smallpox rode high, and in 1850 the matter was
taken up by the Epidemiological Society of London, whose report enabled Lord Lyttleton to get a Bill passed in 1853 imposing
the drastic provision that every infant born in England and
Wales should be vaccinated within three months of birth. After
that the story is complicated, for the severity of Parliament's
action excited opposition. The development of the service was
assisted by researches instigated by John Simon from within
the government. But the fact remains that the researches of
private societies had induced, and the motions of private members of Parliament had initiated, one of the most drastic, and
ultimately one of the most successful, prophylactic policies
founded on compulsion that any modern State had as yet put
its hand to.

In the matter of vaccination the initiative was largely undertaken by medical societies; it might, however, in certain circumstances be undertaken on medical grounds by individuals. In
1850 T. Wakley, the editor of the *Lancet*, began an attack on the
adulteration and pollution of food, and in 1860 an independent
Liberal member named William Scholefield managed to get an
Act passed which, amongst other things, permitted local authori-

ties to appoint a public analyst. This was tightened by the Acts of 1875 and 1879, the last of which made the appointment of analysts compulsory.

In this case, as in the case of compulsory vaccination, the point of departure was professional, but in other cases, even in things medical, it could be wholly philanthropic. For instance, one of the scandals of mid-nineteenth-century England was the state of the workhouse hospitals, where paupers were supposed to be nursed by paupers and conditions were often unspeakable. William Rathbone, who was very definitely one of the philanthropic élite of Liverpool, turned his attention in 1861 to the nursing of the sick poor and invoked the aid of Florence Nightingale. He opened a Training School and Home for Nurses in Liverpool and in 1865 managed to induce the vestry to allow him to introduce twelve trained nurses from St Thomas' Hospital into the Workhouse Infirmary. Miss Nightingale was able to extend the movement to London. In this she was helped by two things: by a scandal, the report of the inquest on the death of a pauper Timothy Daly, and by the skilled advice and assistance of H. B. Farnall, the Poor Law Inspector for the metropolitan district. The matter was possibly delayed and complicated by a change of government, but it resulted in the Metropolitan Poor Act of 1867, and the provision of better hospitals. This was the beginning of a general reform which went on until by 1897 the employment of pauper nurses in any workhouse hospital was forbidden.

If, however, the initiative that led to legislation and the assumption of new executive powers could come from the medical expert or the philanthropist, it could also come from ordinary individuals in the grip of untoward circumstances which they believed the public power could remedy. An outstanding example of this came in 1866 when the pressure of the cattle plague caused a combination of country gentlemen to force on an unwilling government the Cattle Diseases Prevention Act, which made the slaughter of diseased animals compulsory.

But perhaps more significant are those cases where the results of the industrial revolution, or of the population explosion, led ordinary men to require an extension of action by the state.

For instance, one of the results of the industrial revolution was the pollution of the atmosphere. Parliament took an interest in the problem of smoke as early as in 1819, and an Act of 1847 empowered town authorities to take action against smoke nuisances. But really effective action probably only came after 1862 when a select committee of the House of Lords was appointed on the motion of Lord Derby to examine complaints by landowners in Lancashire and Cheshire, who were mainly Conservatives, on the damage done to the countryside by the local manufacturers of chemicals, who were all Liberals, by the emission of fumes from their factories. As a result an Act was passed in 1863 which instituted a control over the amount of acid that was allowed to escape. The inspectors accumulated technical knowledge on the subject and became a living department of government; there developed new demands for a more extensive control and the Act of 1863 was followed by a series of Acts called the Alkali Acts, which are of considerable importance in relation to the problem of the application of science to the problems of government.

If a devastated countryside forced on men's attention the results of the uncontrolled manufacture of chemicals, the stench that penetrated many towns in summer must have made it impossible for them to forget another disagreeable result both of the industrial revolution and of the population explosion, the increasingly filthy state of the rivers, particularly of the Thames, which was the subject of constant gibes in *Punch*. The problem was complicated by the difficulty of disposing of sewage, indeed, as drainage got better the pollution of rivers got worse. The matter was the subject of constant discussion. In 1862 and 1864 the House of Commons appointed select committees to consider the problem, and in 1865 and 1868 there were Royal Commissions to consider the pollution of rivers, but a River Pollution Act did not come till 1876. Probably the right scientific knowledge was not available. But something was done, at very considerable expense, for the Thames. As has been seen in 1855 the Metropolitan Board of Works came into existence and set their hands to draining London. The Thames was embanked, and main sewers were built with intercepting sewers on each side of the Thames to carry the sewage down below London, where outfall sewers discharged it into the estuary at ebb-tide,

eleven and thirteen miles respectively below London Bridge.
The northern outfall works were completed in 1864 and the
southern opened in 1865. Meanwhile in 1857 the Thames Con-
servancy Act had set up a corporate body to handle the rights
and duties which the Crown and the City of London had had
over the lower Thames. This body was mainly concerned with
the Thames as a navigable river, but the Thames Navigation
Act of 1866 not only extended this task to the upper river, but
also gave them the duty of scavenging the upper river, that is
of pulling out of the river the dead cats and other objects that
had been casually thrown into it, and of prosecuting such authorities as tried to discharge sewage into the Thames above
London.

It might have been thought that the Acts protecting labour
or public health would have been matched by laws at least as
effective, for the development of public education. At first sight
indeed it would have seemed likely that there was a greater
chance of development in education. Probably more people were
interested in education than in the problems of health or labour.
Many people were indeed prepared to subscribe quite considerable sums to build and maintain schools, and there were others
who disapproved of the state interfering between employer and
employed in industry, yet believed it had a duty to provide education for those who could not afford it.

Unfortunately in mid-Victorian England there remained a
very general distrust of any system of state-controlled compulsory
secular education. Moreover while men remained interested in
popular education for purely religious reasons the most powerful
secular reasons for desiring to educate the poor, the fear of the
menace to society of the barbarous and disorderly masses, began
to lose its urgency in the quieter and more prosperous conditions
of the 1850s and 1860s. Accordingly there was not a strong
enough demand for the development of public education to
overcome prejudice and make public legislation practicable,
while private members' Bills on education were notoriously
doomed to failure. Therefore the government developed to an
extraordinary extent, not by legislation, but by Privy Council
minutes, a system of popular education, with the help of the various
denominations, the only real point of contact with Parliament

being the vote of the money to be used. The system so created was more extensive and more effective than is often believed. It was nonetheless inadequate and had to be consolidated and extended by the Education Act of 1870, which did at long last supply a place in school for every child. In this case, if in this case only, the consolidation was obviously imposed by the sense of the challenge of advancing democracy caused by the passage of the Act of 1867.

There were, however, some groups of children for whom in the earlier phase even the opponents of state education agreed that the government had educational responsibilities, there were those whom 'destitution, vagrancy or crime casts upon its hands', and legislation on their behalf was practicable. There were pauper children, for whom provision was supposed to have been made by the new Poor Law of 1834. However, little was done for them until Sir James Graham, as Home Secretary, got a measure passed to provide schools for them in 1844. There were, also, delinquent children. In 1845 and 1846 Monckton Milnes busied himself in trying to keep children out of prison, and in 1854 got an Act passed establishing reformatory schools. And there were also vagrant children, for whom industrial schools were provided by a series of Acts which start in 1857.

In order to satisfy the needs of middle class people Parliament took steps to try to secure that existing educational endowments were effectively used, and something was done for technical education. For instance, in 1835 William Ewart had got a select committee appointed to enquire into the question of popular education in art and design, and from 1837 a grant had been made for schools of design, while in 1853, after the Great Exhibition, the Science and Art Department was created to handle education in those subjects.

The educational achievement of these years is of course defective, and Britain was to pay dearly for the failure. Still it is not such a blank as is sometimes suggested, there was something on which a consolidated system could be based after 1870. Perhaps it would have been better if there had not been, for what there was perpetuated the denominational difficulty and helped to make advance very slow. All this is perhaps in significant contrast to the development of the powers of the state which did not touch spiritual matters, but affected unavoidable physical conditions such as the conditions under which men and women lived, and under which they laboured, and to these may perhaps be added another group of laws designed to control another important set of practical concrete problems of urgent importance, the conditions under which they travelled.

These problems pressed for regulation for two reasons. First, as a result of the population explosion a large number of people had to leave the overcrowded land of their birth, particularly if it was Ireland, and pass overseas. This meant that the shippers of a place like Liverpool had on their hands a very large number of peculiarly defenceless passengers. Secondly, from the 1830s onwards men in Britain were developing a revolutionary form of transport, the steam-driven railway train. The speed and efficiency which steam gave to locomotion was of course one of the most important factors in the development of the industrial revolution, but it required special legislation to fit so novel a factor into an ancient society, and rather careful regulation if people carried at such unprecedented speeds were not from time to time to be grievously mangled and killed. These matters were continually pressed on the consciousness of the public by appropriate scandals, the needs of the poor passengers by intermittent revelations of what had happened in emigrant ships, and the problem of the railways by the reports of railway accidents.

To protect the emigrants a series of Passenger Acts were passed which extend from the beginning of the century till 1855. These are of particular interest because an agent was stationed at Liverpool to put them into force in 1833, before inspectors were appointed under the Factory Act. The railways were regulated by a series of Acts starting in 1840. This Act instituted the railway department of the Board of Trade, who were largely responsible for working out in the course of the century the remarkable safety system for British railways.

Parliament may have been hampered in legislating effectively on this subject by a fairly strong railway lobby. Nevertheless, the effectiveness of the treatment of railways in the nineteenth century is an interesting contrast to the fumbling treatment of roads. The Turnpike Trusts by which many of the roads had been built were gradually ruined by the competition of the railways and it was not easy to find a local authority which could satisfactorily take their place. Probably the right solution was the Highway Districts which could be created under the Highway Act of 1862. But the Home Office, whose responsibility it was, failed to press this solution on the country and the whole matter got out of hand until it was handed over to the Local Government Board in 1872. This was partly because in its handling of many matters the Home Office was apt to be a dead department heartily inclined to let things take their course, but it was also because the expanding force of the community was at that moment working through railways and not roads, and there was no need to create effective highway authorities.

This does not pretend to be an account of all the significant legislation that was passed between 1830 and 1870, not even of all the legislation that added to the discretionary powers of the state. But it seemed necessary to give a sample that was sufficiently massive to show what was happening. For this is the critical period, and many people find it difficult to recognize the fact. They are apt to assume that the middle of the nineteenth century is in general a period of legislative nullity when there was little development in social policy and an increase in the powers of the state was extremely improbable.

I have found that in forming this impression students have often been influenced by the belief that they must fit in something called the 'period of *laissez faire*' between about 1820 and 1870, the last date being often very uncertain, and in this, also, they are often influenced by what is in, on examination, an inaccurate memory of what A. V. Dicey says in his *Law and Public opinion in England during the Nineteenth Century*. I do not myself think the conception of a 'period of *laissez faire*' is helpful. It has just enough truth to enable it to conceal its defects, which are many, and it is an encouragement to error. For instance, it encourages those who use it to assume a consistency of outlook and uniformity of practice in many people over a number of years which is not in accordance with the experience of history or the facts of human nature. It suggests too sharp and complete a change in 1870, or whenever the final date is taken to be. Indeed it seems possible that if the phrase 'the period of *laissez faire'* must be used it should be held that the 'period of *laissez faire'* and the 'period of collectivism' run concurrently like prison sentences, and cover most of the nineteenth century. The phrase also confuses habits of mind and conduct, which have a variety of social and historical explanations, with certain specific theories, and incidentally obscures the fact that some at least of the classical economists were prepared to approve of State interference where necessary to meet social needs and that one side of the teaching of Bentham actually encouraged it. Worst of all it tends to divert men's attention towards theory and away from the most powerful factor involved, the impact of particular circumstance.

For I would suggest that what happened between 1830 and 1870, or between 1820 and 1880 for that matter, is, clearly, the immediate result of the reactions of a large number of different people, some of whom I have mentioned by name, many of whom I have not, to the problems which the circumstances of their day presented to them. What they thought about these circumstances was no doubt conditioned by their principles, Tory or Radical, Economist or Benthamite, Christian or Medical, and by their professional training or experience, and by their temperaments, sensitive, missionary or negative. What they thought affected what they did, but a preponderant factor in any decision they had to make was always the need to find a practical solution to the immediate problem which necessity, or their sense of humanity, presented to them; and that need might easily override preconceived principles.

Since what was done was not directed by systematic thought the results of the period between 1830 and 1870 were chaotic. England was parcelled out into districts, each erected to serve a particular purpose. There were boards of guardians, boards of health, highway boards and, after 1870, school boards. There were also older units, counties, boroughs as reformed by the Act of 1835, and parishes with vestries. The boundaries of the districts controlled by the *ad hoc* authorities did not always correspond with the county boundaries, or with those controlled by other authorities existing for different purposes. Since much had been done by local Act or by adoptive legislation the standards of what was done in various parts of the country were very uneven.

At the centre, government by board and committee was evolving slowly into government by ministry; but in several departments the evolution was not complete, it was not always clear where ministerial responsibility lay and there were still relatively independent civil servants, like Sir John Simon. The distribution of the work of government was largely hugger-mugger. The control of the new services, when it was no longer entrusted to independent commissions, was often enough thrown into one of two common administrative ragbags, the Privy Council or the Home Office. The differentiation of function between government offices, as between the Home Office and the Board of Trade, was often arbitrary and unintelligible.

Yet in spite of the confusion it seems to be quite clear what was happening. To most mid-nineteenth-century Britons the modern, powerful, all-controlling state with its intrusive officials armed with drastic executive powers and wide administrative discretions was something which existed in Prussia or in France, but not in England. And here it was growing unperceived in their midst. There were the officials. There were commissioners, unpaid and paid, and assistant commissioners. There were inspectors and sub-inspectors or superintendents and inspectors of nuisances. There were local registrars working under the Registrar-General. There were the officials of the *ad hoc* bodies, and of the boroughs. And there were the police, for after 1856 there had to be a police force in every part of England and, according to Maitland, Parliament 'heaped powers and duties upon police constables' that were not connected with the maintenance of public order, or the prevention of crime. The powers which the police received to enable them to carry out these tasks were wide, particularly if you take account of what a magistrate could do, acting solely on police information.

For Parliament had not been afraid to delegate extensive discretionary powers to public servants, and to enforce obedience by very sharp penalties. The Factory Act of 1833 empowered inspectors to make regulations for factories, to promote complaints of breaches of them, to try the offenders and to impose penalties. This extraordinary concentration of power was modified in the Act of 1844, but that did not mean that the tendency to grant drastic powers had disappeared. In fact it was reinforced by the suggestions of two of the most ruthless spirits that can inhabit the human breast, the spirit inspired by practical philanthropy and that instructed by applied science. For instance in 1853 Shaftesbury proposed a Bill which would have given the police power to bring before the magistrates children found in a state of vagrancy in the streets, that they might be consigned to suitable institutions and so removed 'from the corrupting influence of their parents', who might, however, be asked to contribute to the expenses of their education.

Shaftesbury's proposal did not become law, but the benevolent did not abandon their pursuit of vagrant children, or supposedly vagrant children. In the Industrial Schools Act of 1857 a provision was inserted granting powers for the arrest of vagrant children and their commitment to an industrial school. For this Act two philanthropic Tories, C. B. Adderley and Stafford Northcote, seem to have been responsible. Apparently the measure was not effective, and it was replaced in 1861 by an extraordinary statute (24 & 25 Vic., c.113) which gave to 'any person' (*sic*) the right to bring before the justices—that is two justices acting together in petty sessions, or in certain cases one magistrate acting alone—any child apparently under fourteen years of age whom he claimed to be a beggar or vagrant as defined in the Act. If the magistrates—or magistrate—were satisfied that the information about the child was true they, or he, could commit him to an industrial school till he was fifteen years old.

The sweeping powers which this Act were likely to give to the police were noticed, and objected to, at the time. Lord Robert Cecil (later Lord Salisbury and Prime Minister) moved the excision of the decisive clauses when the Bill was in committee in the House of Commons. He said he could only characterize the Bill as 'worthy of the meridian of Paris and Berlin'. 'The 9th clause gave a power to a single justice to send a child to an industrial school and imprison him there for eight years. One of the offences for which such a sentence could be passed was that of begging, which at present was punished by an imprisonment of three months only. Another was that of frequenting the company of reputed thieves and the proof of that offence having been committed was to depend upon the information of "any" person.' The answer of Sir George Cornewall Lewis, the Liberal

Home Secretary, was tart and virtuous. 'All the arguments of the noble Lord had been repeated half a dozen times before. There was no new principle in the Bill. It was only a development of the existing law, was promoted by persons of the most philanthropic views and was intended not for the punishment but for the advantage of the children who were made subject to it.' Lord Robert Cecil's amendment failed and the Act was passed.

If, however, the plans of persons of the 'most philanthropic views' led to the arming of public authorities with wide discretionary powers, so did those of medical men. As has been said an Act was passed in 1853, as a result of a report of the Epidemiological Society of London, which made vaccination compulsory for all infants born in England and Wales within three months of birth. In 1867 this was sharpened by a very unusual provision for cumulative punishments on defaulters until the cause of offence was removed. These Acts were, however, surpassed in ruthlessness by the Contagious Diseases Acts of 1864, 1866 and 1867. They empowered the police in certain towns to lay an information against any woman that she was a common prostitute. She would then be summoned and either bullied into signing a 'voluntary submission', which would mean that she would have to undergo a series of medical examinations for venereal disease, or she could be brought before a magistrate who could compel her to submit to examination. The magistrate needed only to rely on police evidence that she was what they said she was. If infected, she would be consigned to a hospital under what were prison conditions. The towns in question were naval seaports and garrison towns and the Acts were passed at the behest of the naval and military authorities. But, as the petitions in their favour show, they were supported by many eminent medical men, and there existed an association to promote their extension to the whole kingdom. John Simon opposed this extension. His researches showed that venereal disease was not as widely diffused among the population as was believed, and he thought the extension impracticable.

Both the Vaccination Acts and the Contagious Diseases Acts overreached themselves. The Vaccination Acts gave force to the Anti-Vaccination movement and the law was modified. Josephine Butler fought an heroic campaign against the Contagious

Diseases Acts, and they were at last repealed in 1886. Such Acts, however, show what spirits were abroad. The milder compulsions and discretions remained and no doubt passed into long standing departmental practice such as were complained of in the case of the *Local Government Board* v. *Arlidge* in 1915, practices which went back to the Poor Law Board before 1871.

It would be interesting to discover the date when instructed observers began to see what was happening. John Morley published his *Life of Richard Cobden* in 1881, and in that book, where he is discussing Cobden's attitude to labour legislation in the 1840s, he says, with apparent surprise, of his own day: 'We find the rather amazing result that in the country where Socialism has been less talked about than in any other country in Europe, its principles have been most extensively applied.' In his lectures on *The Constitutional History of England,* Maitland produced an extraordinarily percipient lecture on the state of public law in 1887-8 in which he discusses the great powers granted to the executive by the legislature, and the whole development was summed up in Dicey's *Law and Opinion . . . during the Nineteenth Century* published in 1905. But I think it was not till much later that men began to talk seriously about the need for creating special institutions to give the individual protection in those issues in which the common law no longer protected him. It might be held that to this day he has not actually been given this protection.

The growth in the power of the state is likely to lead to the growth in the power of the expert, and in the second half of the nineteenth century a new element was added to the knowledge which some experts brought to their task. It was indeed provided by the relevant discoveries of the natural scientists. Before 1850 very little reliable scientific knowledge had in fact been relevant to the problems which administrators and legislators had to tackle, nor for that matter were there many trained scientists who could be recruited for the public service. There were, it is true, engineers and there were medical men, and there were a few geologists or chemists, like the invaluable Dr Lyon Playfair. Officers from the Royal Corps of Engineers were of use in the railway department of the Board of Trade in trying to discover the causes of railway accidents and in framing safety regulations, but it seems probable that they were as much directed in this work by common sense as by any professional knowledge that they possessed. Medical men were of great use in the movement for public health, but this was rather because they were careful and systematic observers than because they could bring any relevant scientific knowledge to the work. Indeed, current conceptions about the nature of disease, or the way in which it was transmitted, based as they were upon such ideas as 'spontaneous generation', or belief in 'pernicious effluvia', were completely astray.

In many ways this had not mattered. What had mattered was the realization of the fact that there was a close relationship between dirt and a contaminated water supply, and disease. This could be established by a review of the evidence and the collection of statistics, and with the knowledge so acquired it was possible to go forward in the right direction still talking nonsense about what disease was, or how it spread. Chadwick certainly did what he did in ignorance of the scientific facts on which his work was based. What he called 'scientific legislation' was legislation based upon research, the collection of statistics and possibly on experiment. It was not legislation based on the relevant results of important scientific discoveries. It would therefore be best, for the sake of clarity, to call Chadwick's ideal not 'scientific legislation' but 'experimental legislation'.

With the advent of Simon there came a change. Simon was a distinguished medical man, and in the enquiries he set going he used other distinguished medical men; and what was more important, Pasteur's work, which gave a much sounder knowledge of what disease was and how it was communicated, became available in England about 1865. Simon adopted the new ideas eagerly, promoted experiments to test them and to discover their relevance to the development of work on public health. This was of course considerable both in the treatment of infectious diseases and in the location and planning of hospitals.

In this case scientific discoveries could teach the framers of social policy what they could not have learnt from enlightened common sense, or uninstructed research. There is another example of this tendency in the Alkali Acts, the series of Acts already mentioned, which began in 1863 and had as their object the control of the fumes which the chemical manufacturers of Cheshire and Lancashire were emitting from their factory chimneys. In this case a branch of public policy was only made possible by the previous discoveries of scientists, and depended for its development on the researches of a distinguished scientist. The trouble, of which in the first instance complaints had been made, was caused by hydrochloric acid, and it could only be brought under control if it was possible to test accurately the amount of acid coming from the chimneys of a particular firm at a particular time. Moreover this was an industry in which much capital was invested and which employed a good many men, and it would not have been practical politics to have proposed control unless there existed a method by which the acid could be retained without imposing a crippling loss on the manufacturer. Fortunately both these things could be done in 1863, and a man was available who could put the requisite knowledge to use. The first Act was to be enforced by one inspector and four sub-inspectors. The inspector was Dr Angus Smith, a distinguished chemist, and he was able both to develop an accurate method of testing the fumes emitted, and to encourage manufacturers to adopt a process which turned the acid, which had been lavished over the countryside, to profitable use.

The service followed the line of development of other services. It had its technical disappointments and frustrations and its difficulties with the Treasury; but, largely under the guidance of Smith, it did develop and extend its sphere of operations. More legislation followed and there was a Royal Commission in the 1870s. The number of inspectors increased and Smith became chief inspector. The control was extended to deal with other forms of manufacture and other noxious vapours. The work was not altogether successful. The increase in the number of factories was inclined to negate the results of the reduction in the proportion of noxious vapour emitted by one factory. These Acts were, indeed, only the beginning of a long and difficult battle; but the important point is that it was a battle that could not have been begun unless the relevant scientific discoveries had been made, and could not have been carried on at all without the services of a highly skilled chemist. A new and important element had entered into the organization of public policy. It presented almost illimitable possibilities, but it presented new difficulties, or perhaps an intensification of difficulties which were present from the moment the initiation of public policy passed into expert hands.

If a scientist was going to work in the public service he would have to work with non-scientists, who would have to co-operate with him, be responsible for him, and decide how many of his demands on the public were tolerable—worth the expense they might involve or the distress they might inflict on those who might be their victims. Yet, without his technical training, they might not be able to follow his line of reasoning and, what is more important, test the soundness of his conclusions. This might not matter when the subject was uncontroversial and obscure as was the case with the Alkali Acts, or when decision turned on the results of a fairly large body of unassailable scientific doctrine. But where this was not so, when the subject was well publicized and controversial, or when the technical experts disagreed, then it might be necessary for those who were not technically skilled to decide between those who were highly skilled on a very difficult point. This possibility could, and can, present a very difficult and dangerous situation. Nowadays it is likely to be worked out behind locked doors, whereas in the nineteenth century the matter was more likely to be fought out in a public controversy in the press and in Parliament.

The danger of this method was demonstrated by a tragic episode which took place about the time that the first Alkali Acts were getting under way. In the third quarter of the century great changes were going forward in the design of battleships. First the armoured, then the iron or steel ship, was taking the place of the old wooden battleship; steam was replacing sail, and guns in turrets the old broadside. The great pioneer in the use of turrets was a certain Captain Cowper Coles, an officer of the Royal Navy who had had experience of mounting heavy guns on rafts in the Crimean War. As his ideas developed he became anxious to build a battleship with guns mounted in this fashion. In order to present a small target, while she herself had a wide range of fire, she would have to have a very low free-board, but she would also have to be equipped for both steam and sail in order to keep up with the fleet and have the cruising range which the Admiralty demanded. The designers of the Admiralty, the chief of whom was one E. J. Reid, resisted Coles's designs and insisted on building ships with a high free-board, in order that they might be seaworthy. A lively controversy followed. Coles attacked the Admiralty designers with all the arguments and invective, the talk of 'hide bound officials', 'red tape' and 'the circumlocution office', which are normally of use in attacking a government department. Reid replied with a freedom which would not be permitted to an official nowadays and talked apparently of becoming a member of the House of Commons, where the matter had been raised.

For some time Coles made no headway. Then in the American Civil War the *Merrimac* and the *Monitor,* ships built on lines which resembled Coles's ideas, proved more than a match for ships of conventional design. Shortly afterwards Coles's turrets were subjected to some experimental tests, which were successful, and in 1866 he was given his chance. He was instructed to build a ship, the *Captain,* according to his design. She was commissioned in April 1870, went two successful voyages, and then, early on the morning of 7 September, was struck by a squall, heeled over, could not recover, and plunged to the bottom with her crew of five hundred men, except for seventeen who were on deck and able to get clear.

The responsibility for this disaster can be variously distributed. The responsibility for the design lay with Messrs Lairds and with Coles, who himself went down with the ship. It is possible that the Admiralty should not have accepted her, as her free-board was actually less than it was in the specification. It is possible that they should have sent to her captain, Troubridge, certain calculations about her centre of gravity which Messrs Lairds had asked for, though it seems very unlikely that that would have made much difference. Technically the responsibility lay with Childers, the First Lord of the Admiralty, and there were those who wished to push this home, for he was already at issue with important figures at the Admiralty, where he had been a reformer and had disturbed the peace and incomes of a good many veterans.

But it is difficult to take his responsibility seriously. The issue had been a technical one and Childers was primarily a financier. Childers certainly believed in the ship, and paid dearly for his belief, for he had contrived to secure that his son, who was a midshipman, should serve aboard her. But the ship had actually been ordered by an earlier administration, before he became First Lord of the Admiralty. There might seem an analogy with the fate of the great airship R101 in 1930, but in that case the political interference had been more culpable and the responsibility of the minister greater. In fact, if it is necessary to attribute responsibility in 1870 to anyone, perhaps it should be attributed to the ignorant opinion in press and Parliament which presumed to pronounce on a highly technical matter, or to the politicians who had yielded to that opinion. That at least seems to be the sense of the bitter words in the finding of the court martial which followed the incident, words which are repeated on the plaque commemorating the dead on the wall of St Paul's, an unusual breach of the decorum that normally shrouds memorials.

Even so, it is difficult to say that Coles should not have appealed to the public. He had an important point to make, and it is difficult to see how he could have made it in any other way. Nor can it be asserted with absolute confidence that neither Parliament nor ministers ought to have attended to him; there might be danger in the doctrine that the only technical opinion ever to be considered is the opinion of the senior technical officer in the government service, nor does it seem certain that it is best to settle these matters behind closed doors without allowing the general public a chance to intervene. Within the civil service itself there may be forces which might contrive to stifle the deployment of technical opinion, forces for which the right kind of publicity might be a salutary control.

This possibility is suggested by the fate of John Simon. To that fate, however, a contribution was made from outside the civil service. Its source is indeed ironical. It demonstrates a possible limitation on the working of the principle of experimental legislation, or perhaps on the minds of those who may use that method. Chadwick had made great claims for the use of a method which based legislation upon facts ascertained by

strict and careful enquiry. He claimed that such enquiries almost always revealed the fact that men's common assumptions
on almost any given subject were wrong. At first no doubt he
acted on his principle, and conducted his enquiries with a reasonably open mind. But after a time his opinions became clear.
He came to certain conclusions about the proper way to handle
the problems of public health, and he did not alter them again;
if he enquired it was rather to confirm than to explore. What he
felt he had to do was not to reconsider what he knew to be
right, but rather to fight for it against the forces of dirt, prejudice and corruption that confronted him on every side. His
opinions had hardened from the tentative conclusions of an ex-
perimentalist into the fighting creed of a crusader.

Unfortunately this had happened before Pasteur's work became available, and he was not prepared to consider the new
doctrine about the nature of disease. In this refusal he found
himself in sympathy with another old crusader, Florence Nightingale. She also saw no reason to revise her opinions, or to consider new knowledge. As she wrote to Chadwick in 1871: 'What
we want most now is *not to know but to do.*' When, therefore
Simon's practice came to be influenced by Pasteur's doctrine
these two began to be increasingly critical of it. Normally he
could have weathered this trouble, but there came a point when
they launched a joint attack on him at a moment when his whole
position was in danger.

The nature of that danger can only be understood by looking
back at the history of the civil service, and also at the slow evolution of a truly Parliamentary Executive. When the great administrative pioneers, such as Chadwick and Kay-Shuttleworth,
were recruited the whole civil service was recruited by direct
political nomination. That was how they got their jobs. But unfortunately others, who were not quite as valuable to the country, also got their jobs by nomination. There were for instance
unlikely youths whose orthography had to be carefully tested
before they were entered into the work of an office, and whose
main anxiety after admission was to keep the duns away from
their official chiefs. Or there were well connected men of fashion
who were given appointments for which they had no obvious
aptitude, and in the duties of which they showed no obvious

interest. Probably the number of really scandalous appointments has been exaggerated, but the whole system was a scandal and many people were anxious to reform it. To determine the lines which reform might take Gladstone, as Chancellor of the Exchequer, instructed Sir Stafford Northcote and Sir Charles Trevelyan to carry out an enquiry. They produced their famous report in 1854.

The Northcote-Trevelyan report proposed two related objectives. They wished to replace nomination by entry by competitive examination and to staff the public offices with a more respectable type of civil servant who would be given more intelligently conceived duties. Where the new upper civil servants were to come from seems to be made reasonably clear from a letter by Jowett, then a tutor at Balliol, which is appended to the report. He commends, from a public point of view, the system of entry by competitive examination and adds: 'though a subordinate aspect of it, I can not help feeling, as a College Tutor, its great importance to the University, supplying as it does to well-educated young men a new opening for honourable distinction'. It was a cry from a tutor's heart. Both Oxford and Cambridge had grown in numbers since the beginning of the century, both were at least partially reformed and each was therefore producing more 'well-educated young men' than ever before. This was excellent, but when they had completed their course how should they earn a living? Probably fewer men than in the past were prepared to take holy orders as a matter of course. The Bar accepted a good many of them, but not a few of the most intelligent after reading in chambers very reasonably found law exceedingly repugnant, and for such men the expanding civil service and inspectorate provided a heaven-sent opportunity.

The politicians were reluctant to give up nomination, and open competition for entry into most of the Home Civil Service had to wait till 1870, but long before that time men who had distinguished themselves at Oxford and Cambridge were finding their way in, and when anyone got in he drew others after him. For instance, R. W. Lingen, a past fellow of Balliol and a friend of Jowett, entered the Education Office; in 1849 he succeeded Kay-Shuttleworth as its permanent head, and he, we are told,

relied on the recommendations of Jowett in appointing exam-
iners and inspectors from Oxford, using for the same purpose
W. H. Thompson of Trinity, for Cambridge. As a result of this
policy no less than four successive permanent heads of the Education Office—Lingen, Sandford, Cumin and Kekewich—were
Balliol men.

It would be interesting to know how far this penetration went,
and to learn to what extent the Scottish Universities, Trinity
College, Dublin, or the University of London took their share.
It would be also interesting to know whether a common educational origin had an effect on the entrants into public offices in
mid-century, which in turn influenced public policy. It is possible to speculate. It is possible to guess that younger men, whose
experience of adult life had been almost exclusively academic
in the Oxford and Cambridge of those days, would have a less
clear sense of mission, a less positive view of what they felt ought
to be done, than the kind of people whom the Whigs appointed
in the 1830s who were often older men who had already made
their mark in radical polemics before they were recruited. Moreover the kind of education an able man would have received
in the mid-nineteenth-century Oxford or Cambridge might not
have prepared him very well for administrative problems that
required a knowledge of, or even a respect for, natural science;
nor perhaps would it have given him the type of mind that was
much interested in social research. On the other hand it would
have enhanced his powers of clear thought, lucid expression and,
what might be most important, effective criticism; and if his
University career had been distinguished it might have given
him considerable self-confidence. If these guesses are correct it
seems possible that here was a source of valuable public servants,
but perhaps of men more likely to criticize other peoples'
schemes than to produce their own, to administer effectively,
and above all economically, the laws entrusted to them rather
than to want to innovate. Such men might perhaps be called
'literal' rather than 'experimental' administrators.

It is, however, wrong to speculate on what should be a matter
for research, and it must be wrong to generalize too freely. There
is a danger that the picture should be too much influenced by
the known characteristics of certain powerful characters who did

come from Oxford at this time. R. W. Lingen, the first of the Balliol Secretaries of the Education Office was one of the ablest of these. Of him the *Dictionary of National Biography* says that as Secretary 'his strength lay perhaps not so much in his capacity to make changes as in his ability to negative claims on the public purse'. It was a capacity he seems to have shown to the full when, helped by Robert Lowe, vice-president of the Education Committee, and also at one time Fellow of Magdalen College, Oxford, in 1862 he cut Kay-Shuttleworth's developments in public education down to size using for the purpose the revised code and the system of 'payment by results'. In 1869 Lingen carried his antiseptic qualities to the position of permanent Secretary of the Treasury to find congenial company, Bob Lowe as Chancellor of the Exchequer and as Prime Minister another Oxford man, and strenuous advocate of economy, W. E. Gladstone. In his new position Lingen helped to form part of the ring that formed round John Simon when at last he was brought to bay. It is only fair to say that, whatever he had done in education, Lowe, whatever position he held, was ever the friend of Simon. But he could not save him.

The closing of the ring round Simon was, immediately, the result of the reorganization of the department for which he himself had worked, even if its effectiveness came from the general acceptance of the doctrine of ministerial responsibility. After the Act of 1866 it became increasingly necessary for the various authorities concerned with public health to be combined in one organization and under one minister. The Royal Commission on the sanitary laws which sat from 1869-71 recommended this, Simon himself desired it and in an unhappy moment suggested that the work of the various health authorities could be combined with that of the Poor Law Board. The recommendation was put into effect by the Act of 1871 which erected the Local Government Board. Simon had envisaged what would have been in fact a ministry of health with a dynamic policy, and no doubt with himself as secretary. He did not become secretary. The place of secretary was given to J. W. Lambert, Secretary of the Poor Law Board. Lambert was not in fact a University man, but he was an able and a devoted administrator, rather of the Lingen type, a favourite with Gladstone. He was clear that a technical expert in a government office should be there to give advice when he was asked, and not to take the initative in policy, and that Simon should occupy that position.

Simon's collapse was rapid. It seems probable that at this moment Chadwick and Florence Nightingale contrived to poison the mind of the minister, Stansfeld, against him. Certainly Simon was not allowed contact with Stansfeld. Nor was he allowed for a time even to publish the reports by means of which he had influenced the public. The policy which the new Local Government Board followed was that of the old Poor Law Board. It was guided by what Simon called in his bitterness 'secretarial commonsense'—that is common sense which is primarily concerned with the smooth and controlled working of the administrative machine, and is not interested in the possibility of a progressive policy. Simon felt the futility of his position acutely, lost heart and retired in 1876. He was only 56, but there was nothing more for him though his life was cruelly prolonged till 1904.

It has been said by those who have been in a position to know that the imposition of the policy and ways of thought of the Poor Law Board or the Local Government Board put back the development of a policy of public health for about thirty years. Indeed there can be little doubt that the loss of Simon in his maturity, Simon who had probably become the leading expert in Europe on these matters, cost many lives and caused many opportunities to be thrown away. Nevertheless there is something to be said on the other side. Different though Simon was both in temperament and approach from Chadwick, the place which he claimed in the business of government was essentially the same, and the methods which he wished to use were essentially the same also. Simon wished to initiate policy, he also wished to be able to appeal outside his office, and over the heads of the government, to the public to gain support for his policy. These were claims with which any permanent head of a department and any Parliamentary minister could legitimately quarrel. It is significant that it was Simon's position in the department and not the fact that he was a scientist that provided the issue between Simon and Lambert. Angus Smith of the Alkali Acts also came under the Local Government Board. He was at least as considerable a scientist as Simon, and he was developing a policy even more completely based on scientific research. Yet Smith got on reasonably well with Lambert, who clearly respected his scientific knowledge. That does not mean that with a stronger minister than Stansfeld, a less masterful permanent head than Lambert, or a more understanding Prime Minister than Gladstone, this tragedy might have been postponed. Perhaps the position might have been recovered if Disraeli, Prime Minister after 1874, had been the friend to public health he pretended to be. But, whatever happened, it seems probable that the position Simon claimed must in the end have raised questions which would be answered in a way Simon would dislike.

The fact is that it was going to be impossible to domesticate these independent pioneer administrators, who had been so important in the second and third quarter of the nineteenth century, to the ways of a government service with a developed organization, professional personnel and a recognized constitutional position in the state, such as had come into existence by the beginning of the fourth quarter of the century. The activities of such men might reasonably be resented by those who had to act as their colleagues in the service, and would not be easy to reconcile with any acceptable constitutional theory. In a Parliamentary system every executive action should be authorized by a minister responsible to Parliament. If an action is imposed upon a minister by a civil servant who has seized the initative the minister cannot be expected to be responsible for it. Moreover it is constitutionally necessary that the law upon which policy is to be based should be the law as passed by Parliament and should be used for the purposes which Parliament intended, and not developed to serve another purpose which no one in Parliament had in mind when it was passed. Anything else makes nonsense of the theory of Parliamentary government and of democracy. In the last resort the only constitutional rule for administration is that it should be 'literal' administration.

It might, therefore, be said that the heroic age of pioneering administrators had been very useful, but that it necessarily came to an end. Chadwick and Simon had been invaluable in their day, but the time had come when public servants must be reduced to a position in which the constitutional proprieties were better observed. The trouble was that it was still difficult both to satisfy the demands of constitutional propriety and at the same time meet the needs of a constantly changing society dependent on an ever developing technology. For instance, it was not always possible to continue to enforce the literal interpretation of an Act of Parliament, which the government would not amend or replace to meet new demands and a rapidly transformed situation. In such a case even the most conservative officials might not be able to keep within the presumed intentions of a Parliament which had long passed into history.

For instance the law passed in 1870 to provide a general elementary education in England increasingly failed to satisfy the demands of the more advanced local educational authorities. Parliament legislated gingerly on such matters as the freeing of State education from fees, or the making of elementary education compulsory for everyone. But Parliament failed to pass an Act which would make provision for an adequate system of public secondary education. Secondary education was, however, what in effect a good many school boards were asking for; consequently the officials of the Education Department, anxious as they were to keep within the terms of the Act, sanctioned a series of grants which really subsidized secondary education. These were all declared to be illegal by the Cockerton judgment in 1900.

That judgment was in fact in part the result of a mine which had been placed and detonated by Robert Morant, then an official in the Education Office, to clear away the educational detritus which impeded the way to a satisfactory educational policy, which should include an Act clearly providing state-aided secondary education such as was passed largely as a result of Morant's pressure from within the office in 1902.

Indeed Morant's activities seem to be very like a reversion to the initiation of policy by crusading pioneering civil servants like Simon or Chadwick or Kay-Shuttleworth. There are differences, of course, but the resemblance is sufficiently close for Morant's background to be of interest. He was an Oxford man, but the Oxford of his undergraduate days was the Oxford inspired by Ruskin, Canon Barnett, T. H. Green and Arnold Toynbee, an Oxford in which a man could acquire a sense of social mission as Morant did, which he was perhaps less likely to have done in mid-nineteenth-century Oxford, when attention was apt to be concentrated on the burning religious issues raised by the Oxford Movement and by Modernism, and an earnest man was more likely to be troubled about the meaning of the thirty-nine articles than the condition of the people. But perhaps what is even more significant is the fact that Morant had entered the office in middle life and was therefore not imbued with its traditions, and with the traditions which the civil service had developed. Perhaps it was because he was thus uninhibited that he was enabled to give English educational policy a fresh start.

If this is so there may be a comparable history in the Local Goverment Board. Lambert had put a stop to innovation by Simon and had created an administrative machine which ran smoothly along the rails prescribed for it. But the demands for the development of public health services did not stop. They were pressed by private societies, by local authorities, by progressive medical officers of health, and in 1908 by Sir Arthur Newsholme, who had been medical officer of health at Brighton, with the result that the wheels moved as swiftly as the times demanded.

If there is anything in this comparison it suggests that if a new age in social policy was beginning it needed new officials to usher it in. But the age of Morant and Newsholme raises problems which I am not prepared to touch.

For 1908 is beyond my terms of reference. It is an era which is essentially different from that which I have been discussing. By 1908 the constitutional changes of the nineteenth century had been completed. The doctrine of ministerial responsibility covered effectively all the executive actions of government servants, and the personal activities of the permanent civil service were restrained by known rules. Party discipline was stricter, the government took a far larger share of the time of the House of Commons and the opportunities for private members were fewer. On the whole the theory of democracy was accepted and with it the doctrine of mandate. And if that doctrine was, as it is always, rather illusory, there was, at least after 1906, a more

See errata page

conscious intention to direct and expand social policy on the part of the government.

Behind this new constitutional and political position there was a wider acceptance of the need and propriety of interference by the state in the social life of the country. Not only were there important organized groups openly working for that end, such as the Labour party or the Fabian Socialists, but there were many more who consciously accepted some form of collectivism as a necessary instrument for social decency and justice, and more still who were advocating policies, or themselves developing services, which must end in the extension of state action. For it is one of the most striking lessons of the twentieth century that the state is the residuary legatee of most of the generous enthusiasms and endeavours of public spirited men and women.

All this makes it essential for this later phase to be considered separately. But it is important that whoever does this should keep the earlier phase in perspective, for many of the problems that are obvious now had their origins then, and many of the problems that became evident then may remain unsolved today. For instance, the problem of delegated legislation and jurisdiction, about which so much has been written since Lord Hewart's book in 1929, had its origins in the 1830s and it is worth-while thinking carefully why the practice started, and why as the system developed no countervailing system, such as that of the ombudsman or the *Conseil d'État,* was devised to control it. On the other hand the problem of the initiative of the expert in the government service, so obvious in the days of Chadwick, may still be not completely solved today, in spite of the fact that it *attach to the* is glozed over by conventions which attack the doctrine of ministerial responsibility. Certainly the problems presented by the conflict on difficult technical matters between the opinions of highly qualified experts remain. There is a very interesting and important example of this issue in the clash between Sir Henry Tizard and Lord Cherwell, just before and during the war of 1939, about which Lord Snow and others have written. Without doubt this problem will recur.

If, however, the mid-Victorian period is considered by itself, the lesson which it seems to teach most eloquently is the great

influence in human affairs of the force of necessity, of the pressure of circumstances. Most intelligent and influential people in
Victorian England believed to a greater or less extent in self-help,
the avoidance of state control, government economy and the
anxious preservation of human freedom. Yet they started to build
one of the most effective systems of state government in Europe,
and they had to do so. Certainly what they did was at every
point directed by human intelligence and moulded by human
ideas. Many different people were involved in this work and
their thought and their characters made a difference to what
was done. If they had been different, or their opportunities and
fortunes had been different, or if other people had taken their
places, what would have been done would have been different.
Some of it might have been better, some worse. Some of it
would have come more slowly, some more quickly. All of it
might have had a different design. But it seems impossible to
doubt that given the circumstances of Britain in the nineteenth
century something resembling what did happen would have happened, whoever the agents available might have been.

For at the end I return to what I said at the beginning. Here
was a community trying to live in an overcrowded island with a
constantly growing population. It was faced by the problems of
ever-increasing urbanization. It had to respond to the challenges
and opportunities of the industrial and scientific revolutions. It
was increasingly enlightened and disturbed by the leaven of
humanitarian and religious feeling which had begun to work in
it in the eighteenth century, and it was subject to the slowly
mounting demands of democracy. Such circumstances made an
increasingly elaborate social policy necessary. Such a policy could
only be put into effect by an increasingly powerful secular state.
Some men may have seen the general direction in which they
were travelling, others certainly did not. It did not matter. It is
to be doubted whether what was coming into existence was
exactly what anyone's principles or prejudices had led him to
desire or to expect, since eighteenth-century optimism, the principle of the ultimate natural identity of human interests, is as
implicit in much of Benthamism as it is in Communism. But
men's intentions had to conform, not to what was recommended

by theory, but to what was demanded by fact, and they were not masters of the future.

If this is true it also is worth-while considering carefully, for many of the necessities which gave this direction to human affairs still press upon us.

Clark, G. S. R. Kitson, 'Statesman in Disguise', *Historical Journal*, vol. 11, no. 1, 1959.

Dicey, A. V., *Lectures on the Relation between Law and Public Opinion in England during the Nineteenth Century*. London, 1905, second ed., 1914, 1962.

Finer, S. E., *The Life and Times of Sir Edwin Chadwick*. London, 1952.

Hart, Judith, 'Nineteenth-Century Social Reform: A Tory Interpretation of History', *Past and Present*, no. 31, July 1965.

Lambert, Royston, *Sir John Simon 1816-1904, and English Social Administration*. London, 1963.

MacDonagh, Oliver, *A Pattern of Government Growth, 1800-60; the Passenger Acts and their Enforcement*. London, 1961.

——, 'The Nineteenth Century Revolution in Government', *Historical Journal*, vol. 1, no. 1, 1958.

Parris, H., *Government and the Railways in Nineteenth-Century Britain*. London, 1965.

Roberts, David, *Victorian Origins of the Welfare State*. New Haven, 1960.

INDEX

Adderley, C. B., 165
Agriculture: agriculturalists' discontent with Tories before 1830, 23; hatred of agricultural protection, 25-6; fortunes after repeal of Corn Laws, 27-8, 37-8; see also Corn Laws and Anti-Corn Law League
Alkali Acts, xi, 158, 169-70
Anti-Corn Law League, 17, 25-6, 30, 41, 42, 146
Argyll, eighth Duke of, 44
Aristocracy: influence over government, 13, 18, 28, 36, 173; hostility towards, 6, 17, 25-6, 30, 35, 68
Arnold, Matthew, 34, 41, 42, 94, 97
Asquith, H. H., 54-5

Bagehot, Walter, 34-5, 37, 97, 145
Balliol College, Oxford, 174, 175-6
Bannerman, Campbell-, Sir Henry, see Campbell-Bannerman, Sir Henry
Baptists, 2, 16, 96
Barnett, S. A., Canon, 179
Beerbohm, Max, 70
Bentham, Jeremy, 140
Benthamism, 34, 163, 182
Bentinck, Lord George, 19
Besant, Mrs Annie, 103
Birkenhead, 150
Birmingham, 10, 40, 45
Blackstone, Sir William, 63, 128-9
Bonham, F. R., 24
Bowring, Sir John, 82
Bradford, 40
Bradlaugh, Charles, 103
Bright, John, 17, 26, 28, 30, 56, 57, 68, 71, 82
Browning, Robert, 34
Buckingham, third Duke of, 18
Buckingham, J. S., 150
Bulgarian atrocities, 45-6, 65-6
Buller, Charles, 64
Bunting, Jabez, 16
Burke, Edmund, 63
Butler, Mrs Josephine, 166
Byron, Lord, 108-10

Calverley, C. S., 34
Cambridge University, 15, 31-2, 33-4, 97-8, 174-5
Campbell-Bannerman, Sir Henry, 51
Canning, George, 22

Captain, H.M.S., loss of, 170-2
Cardigan, seventh Earl of, 18
Cardwell, Edward, 148
Castlereagh, Lord, 21
Catholic Emancipation Act, 21-2
Catholics, Roman, 2, 15
Cattle plague, compulsory slaughter, 157
Chadwick, Sir Edwin, 35, 136-7, 139-43, 145-6, 149, 151-2, 168, 172-3, 177, 179, 181
Chamberlain, Joseph, 45-6, 54-6, 71
Chartists, 20, 31, 40, 90, 121
Charity Organization Society, 135
Childers, H. C. E., 171-2
Christianity: criticism of, 95-6, 102-4, 120; revivalism, 96, 117-18; see also Evangelical Christianity; Missionaries; and names of denominations
Cities, growth of, 8-10
Civil Service, functions and recruitment of, 14, 132, 137-47, 151-3, 164, 167-82
Clough, A. H., 34
Cobden, Richard, 17, 25-7, 30, 41-2, 68, 70, 81-2, 99
Colenso, Bishop, J. W., 95
Coles, Captain Cowper, 170-2
Congregationalists, 17
Conservative Party, 24, 38, 40, 55, 57-8, 59
Constitution, British, 131; see also Aristocracy; Civil Service; Freedom, and liberalism; Government: old conception; Parliament
Contagious Diseases Acts, 166-7
Corn Laws, Repeal of, 25-8, 30, 38, 132
Cory, William, 137
Croker, J. W., 12, 24
Curgenven, Dr J. B., 155

Dalhousie, tenth Earl of, 72
Darwin, Charles, 95, 97
Darwinism, 96, 100, 103, 122
Derby, fourteenth Earl of, 10, 57, 158
Dicey, A. V., 131, 149, 162, 167
Dickens, Charles, 17, 33, 93, 112, 116
Dilke C. W., 69

185